What are People Saying about This Book?

Mike Watson provides a very practical and logical framework to the management of small projects [...] it is practical and entertaining [...] in an area neglected by writers and practitioners alike [...] This book most definitely fills the gap.
Dr. Chris Preece, University of Leeds

Its small format means you can take this book anywhere and use it as a check guide [...] and simply put, this book is about helping people control smaller projects in a logical and effective way, and making the process run smoothly, and is indeed a success in achieving that goal.
Keri Allan, *IEE Engineering Management*, Dec/Jan 2004/05

Managing Smaller Projects

A Practical Guide

Mike Watson

Second Edition

Multi-Media
Publications Inc.
Lakefield, Ontario

Managing Smaller Projects: A Practical Guide
by Mike Watson

Acquisitions Editor: Kevin Aguanno
Typesetting: Tak Keung Sin
Cover Design: Cheung Hoi

Published by:
Multi-Media Publications Inc.
R.R. #4B, Lakefield, Ontario, Canada, K0L 2H0

http://www.mmpubs.com/

ISBN (Paperback): 1-895186-85-4

Published in Canada. Printed in U.S.A.

Second Edition. Revised for the North American marketplace.

Originally published by Project Manager Today Publications in Great Britain: first edition in 1998 and second edition in 2002 (ISBN 1-900391-09-0).

Library and Archives Canada Cataloguing in Publication

Watson, Mike
    Managing smaller projects : a practical guide / Mike Watson.
-- 2nd ed.

ISBN 1-895186-85-4

    1. Project management. 2. Small business. I. Title.

HD69.P75W385 2006   658.4'04   C2006-902471-5

Table of Contents

Dedication

All authors go through highs and lows. I want to thank both Adrian Dooley of The Projects Group plc for pushing me through the lows and my wife Hannah for helping me enjoy the highs.

Foreword

This book is all about helping people to control smaller projects in a logical and effective way, without incurring the high overheads that come with the project management methods, tools and techniques that are now being used so effectively on large projects and within large organisations.

The Smaller Projects (SP) Method is designed for use both by complete newcomers to project management and those with some experience. It is logical and practical so that it can be applied to a single, small project, or to a portfolio of many smaller projects within an organisation.

The danger, especially in larger organisations, is that smaller projects are left to their own devices while ignoring the fact that together they may represent a significant financial risk that is not being effectively controlled. The only safe and effective way of controlling such activities is to apply the principles of project management.

This book takes those basic principles and gives you the basis for your own project control system.

Mike Watson

Introduction

Many of the methods and techniques used in traditional project management look like proverbial sledgehammers when directed at smaller projects. So I set out to devise a system that can be used easily to create a way of controlling smaller projects in any environment. The result is the Smaller Projects (SP) Method which is the basis of this book.

I hesitated to call it SP because it sounds bureaucratic and SP is nothing of the kind. It is designed to make the adoption of the principles of project management as simple as possible. So here you will find:

- The what, why and how of managing smaller projects.

- A series of standard copyright-free forms which you can use, copy or adapt to suit your own environment (see Appendix A).

- Checklists to remind you of the various techniques you could apply at each stage of a project (see Appendix B).

In addition to essential background information, the examples and case studies show how you can begin to take control of your projects right away.

I have deliberately left out topics which are interesting and important in the wider context of project management, but are luxuries in dealing with smaller projects. Hence you will not find such topics as

- Team building and motivation

- Personnel management

- Meetings

- Fact finding

- Creativity and decision-making

- Resolving conflict

Also, because the dividing line between 'small' and 'large' projects is unclear, I have sometimes referred to how a technique might be applied in a 'larger project' without giving further details. This is deliberate as SP is not designed to be all things to all project managers.

The standard forms included in the text and reproduced in Appendix A are yours to use as you wish. There are also two checklists in Appendix B to remind you of the techniques that you should consider at each stage of a project.

I believe that the benefits of adopting the approach given in this book are immeasurable. Use it on your smaller projects and see the difference. But don't take my word for it, read on and form your own judgement.

Managing Smaller Projects: A Practical Guide

CHAPTER ONE

Introducing the SP Method

The problem with defining a project is that the word 'project' is too readily attached these days to activities that are nothing of the kind. We need to establish a definition of a project and its characteristics in order to test any activity to see if it really is a project.

Let's start by defining a project. It is 'the process of carrying out work to achieve a clear objective, usually bringing about change.' This is not very precise, so let's list the usual characteristics of a project:

- Agreed, well defined objectives and end products

- A startpoint and an endpoint

15

- A balance between time, cost and quality
- Many interrelated tasks, often grouped into phases
- A temporary project team brought together for the project
- A multi-disciplinary team
- The involvement of people from other organisations
- It brings about change

These are projects –

- Moving the office to new premises across town
- Creating the company stand at an exhibition
- Creating a name and address system for direct marketing mailings
- Organising the Olympics
- Building a bridge over a river
- Taking the family on a holiday

The above all have the characteristics of projects.

These are **not** projects –

- Running the office reception desk
- Fixing wheel nuts onto a Ford Mondeo
- Producing the month end accounts

These activities are careful repetitions of a standardised process. They are not projects. Many people confuse the performance of routine tasks with projects; in theory there can be a fuzzy dividing line.

However, for all practical purposes, if a job consists of carrying out a well-established set of tasks, in an environment that is well understood and stable, with personnel who are trained and experienced in those tasks, then that job is a routine process. It is not a project. As soon as the set of tasks starts to vary from the standard, or the environment takes on an unclear, or unstable aspect, you may be looking at a 'project.'

Signs of a successful project

How do you recognise a successful project? If you could put a 'Yes' against every one of the following characteristics you would be looking at a successful project:

yes?	
yes	met its business objectives
yes	it delivered its end product on time
yes	it delivered its end product within budget
yes	its end product met all its quality criteria
yes	the customer was happy with the end product
yes	the customer uses the end product
yes	the customer wants us to do more
yes	the project team felt good about it
yes	change during the project was managed effectively

Sales Manager	Project Manager
routine, from year to year	role ends when project ends
no specific dates other than, say month end	start date, end date difficult to predict
stable organisation	temporary project team
needs set of specialist skills	many different skills needed in team
annual budget easily identified	costs very dificult to estimate
work is repetitive and well-known	work often not done before
room to plan within annual budget	time, cost and quality constraints

In practice, however, there are distressingly few projects that score a 'Yes' against every point.

Management skills

We need to round off this discussion of definitions by looking at the skills of project management. Compare the working environment of two managers: a project manager and a line manager (say, the manager of the sales department). There are some interesting differences (see opposite).

You can see that the skills and techniques needed by the project manager are different from those needed by the sales manager. This guide is aimed at putting those skills and techniques into a practical framework so that the project manager improves his or her chances of success.

The need for the SP Method

As a patient being prepared for minor surgery in a hospital operating theatre you would be rather surprised if the medical team called for a brain scan, full DNA typing, and a test for colour-blindness, before removing your appendix. Interesting and valuable though these tests might be, they would be irrelevant for such a small job.

An experienced medical team would know that they might need only to monitor vital and relevant indicators; a novice team might not know which are the vital indicators and which are distractions. The result could be an operation that takes three times as long at four times the cost. Project managers often face similar choices Imagine your reaction if your boss announces that your company has won the contract to organise the Olympics.

Terror and panic might be your first reaction, but for a project of this size you would find many project management methodologies (standardised approaches), techniques, training courses, consultancy firms and software planning tools all geared up to help you. You would immediately recognise that you were faced with the medical equivalent of transplant surgery and would act accordingly.

Now imagine your reaction to the boss saying 'I think we should have a stand at the trade exhibition in Harrogate next month, and I want you to organise it.' Your reaction could be one of excitement, or concern, or minor panic, but without some guidelines, you might try to manage the exhibition project with the same approach as the Olympics. If this happens there are only three possible outcomes: firstly, you will drown in a sea of overheads; secondly, you will give up project management in order to try to get the work done; or thirdly, you will run over budget, work late into the night, and produce a poor end product.

Choosing the right tools

Sorting out the vital few from the trivial many is the prime aim of the smaller projects (SP) method. Its aim is to combine elements of a full blown project management methodology and the simplicity of the back of an envelope. SP focuses on the vital few elements, to the exclusion of the techniques that are appropriate only to larger projects.

A few forms are used to document the vital features of a project. These forms must be kept as simple as possible or else you would not bother using them. A complete set of forms is included in Appendix A. There is no copyright on them, so you can copy them, amend them, or ignore them as you see fit! You can also get copies from the *Project Manager Today* website: www.pmtoday.co.uk.

Other approaches

For large projects there are any number of methods that you can choose to use (see Appendix C).

CHAPTER TWO

Project Initiation

You are ready to begin your project and need to get it off to a good start. This chapter goes through the steps involved.

Most business life is concerned with judgements or trade-offs, assessing a range of possible projects and selecting one to start. There are numerous techniques for making the 'right' decision, but these are outside the scope of SP; SP starts once the decision to initiate a project has been made.

Even on the smallest project, the project manager would be foolish and irresponsible to spring into action as soon as the starting gun is fired. A few minutes thought at this stage will save a lot of heartache. But what do you need to think about? If the project has some unusual characteristics, what can be done with that information?

The first step in any project is to make time to think and to gain a clearer view of the project based on the conclusions.

Strategic project factors

Firstly, think about the Strategic Project Factors. These sound rather grand, but are simply questions addressing specific issues that must be asked at the start of a project so that the strategy for dealing with the project can be identified. Strategy, in this context, simply means the practical approach you will adopt to tackle the project.

The Strategic Factors are listed below. It may well be that no answers are forthcoming. Some of the questions may be too difficult to answer at the outset, so a mechanism must be created to accumulate useful knowledge for a better answer later. For example, an accurate answer to 'How much will it cost?' may have to be deferred until more research has been carried out.

Problems arising during the project are likely to stem from not having asked the questions; the mere act of asking them can draw attention to just how much is unknown, or unclear, about the project.

Once the questions have been asked (and answered as best you can) you will then be in a better position to decide how to approach the project. The Strategic Project Factors are laid out as a series of questions, in eleven groups.

1. Time constraints

- Is there a fixed target date?

- How fixed is it? (Is it really fixed, say, by a change in the law, or is it linked to an unmissable business opportunity, or is someone just trying it on?)

- Who fixed it?

- Are there any other intermediate target dates that must be met?

- Is there a particular start date that must be taken into account?

- Are the time deadlines of a lesser priority than something else (e.g. cost)?

- What else?

- Can a phased implementation be considered? (For example can you finish part of the job by the target date, and clear up the rest later?)

2. Project profile

- Is the reputation of the company, division, management, project manager, or team at stake?

- Who will get to hear about this project?

- Will a failure be public, or is this a simple 'back room' project?

- Will the project be accompanied by publicity, either internal to the company, or in the trade press, or on international satellite television?

- Is there likely to be high-level management interest in this project?

- What will they want to see?

- Will something have to be finished early in order to show success?

3. Costs and benefits

- Has a cost/benefit analysis been carried out? By whom? When? On what basis? Can the project team see it?

- Has anyone attempted to establish costs? How was this done? Do we have to stick to them? Were the assumptions written down? Can we see them?

- Does this project have a payoff? Who said so? On what basis were possible benefit figures established? How can they be measured?

- What are the relative importance of development costs (i.e. project costs) and the costs of using the end product on an ongoing basis? (Is a quick and cheap solution OK, even if it costs a fortune to use, run, maintain, or service?)

4. Business risk

- How badly will the organisation suffer if this project fails, or if the end product fails to live up to expectations? Will the company go bust?

- What could you lose if the project fails? Customers, sales, staff, money?

- Do you need to keep any aspects of this project secret or confidential (from competitors, staff, etc.)? What would happen if they were to find out what we are doing?

- Do you need to involve Legal, Personnel, Staff Counselling, Accounts, Auditors, outside Statutory or Regulatory bodies?

5. Scope of the project

- How big is this project? Measured how – people involved, departments affected, locations, or outside suppliers? How far apart are these people?

- Will the project have to link with other projects? How and when?

- Will the end product have to link with other products being produced elsewhere? Inside the company or outside?

6. Project background

- Is this a totally new business area for the project team? For the organisation?

- Have we done similar things in the past? What happened?

- Are we taking over something that has already been started? Why?

7. Requirements

- Is what we should produce well understood, agreed upon and stable? Especially, will the requirements change during the lifetime of the project?

- Are the requirements designed to be flexible or are they firm and unchangeable?

- Are these requirements written down? Can the project team see them? Will the project team understand them, or are they very technical?

- Will you have to produce a 'prototype' to help identify and understand the requirements?

- How will the prototype be judged?

- Have the requirements been accepted?

8. Involvement

- Is there commitment at high level for this project? How do we know?

- Will resources be made available to help with the project?

- Will they be appropriately skilled, with appropriate authority to make project decisions?

- Do these resources know about this project?

- What other commitments do they have?

- What are the relative priorities?

- How much time can we expect from them?

9. Technology

- Is the technology in place in our organisation right now, with skilled personnel, documentation etc.? If not, when will it arrive in relation to the rest of the project?

- Is a specification available? Can we use something else as a fallback?

- How many suppliers are involved?

- Who will connect the components together?

- Are the components fully compatible?

- How reliable will the technology be? How reliable must it be? Can the reliability be established?

- Will the project team or the eventual users require training in this technology? How will this be done?

- Will the installation of the technology require other changes or installations (new premises, new furniture, new security, new safety measures)?

- Will the delivery of the technological components cause disruption? Are there personnel or union implications?

10. Project team

- How likely is it that the project team will be able to give the necessary time to the project? What else will suffer as a result?

- Will the project require new skills or disciplines? How will this need be met?

- Will recruitment take place, or will sub-contractors or outside suppliers be engaged? Who will control these people?

- What are the training requirements for the project team?

- What other resources might be needed (for example, desks, work benches, travel services, temporary accommodation)?

11. Project management

- How will the project be managed? Will there be regular meetings, reports, or presentations?

- Is the project manager experienced, trained, and available? What can be done to assist the project manager?

- What standards, guidelines, quality systems, and so on must be followed on this project? If any company standards are not to be followed, why not? Has this been agreed?

- Will any particular techniques be used to manage this project (e.g. SP)? What effect might this have on the project management overhead costs?

Using the answers

Once as many answers as possible have been obtained, it might be tempting to dive in and start work. You would certainly be in a stronger position than before, but you must now consider the supreme question of all: 'So What?' OK, so you discover that the technology you depend upon will not be delivered until half way through the project: so what? Does it matter, and if so, in what way? Asking the questions is straightforward. What you do about the answers may stretch your experience, imagination, and general resourcefulness.

So, maybe you could plan to use some other type of technology early in the project, and only rely upon the newer stuff when it arrives later on; or you could build in an allowance for overtime working in the second half of the project; or you could find someone else who already has the newer stuff, and try to do some of your work at their premises; or you could... If you know in advance, you can run the project accordingly; if you are caught out later, you will be reacting to the project, not managing it.

By bringing all these 'strategic' factors out into the open before the project gets under way you can accomplish two key tasks. Firstly, you can document and communicate to all parties the true state of the conditions surrounding the project. Secondly, you can build your project plan taking the conditions into account.

Let's start the planning process, based upon the Strategic Factors.

Developing a strategy

The point of having a strategy is to see the project in its wider context and to be able to see a way of tackling it. Any large problem, when broken down into smaller, more manageable pieces, suddenly loses its mystery. If the breakdown into smaller pieces is based upon an organised set of questions (the strategic project factors), then the project suddenly looks possible and much less daunting.

Phases

The outcome of the Strategic Factors exercise is a list of project pieces. Actually, these 'pieces' have a wide range of names. Most people use terms such as 'phases,' 'stages,' or even 'chunks.' I shall use the word 'phase' to describe a piece of a project.

While on the topic of jargon, I shall call the process of breaking a project down into manageable pieces 'structuring.' (Our American cousins use the term 'chunking' – an unappealing word, but very descriptive of the process!)

Example

Here is an example of using the strategic factors to carry out 'structuring.'

Project 1: Move our office 2 miles across town

The Strategic Factors questions uncovered the following project characteristics:

- **Date constraint:** the old office will be handed back to the landlord on 31st October; we HAVE to be out by that date.

- **Date constraint:** we can gain access to the new office on 1st October, but only for decorating and wiring; we cannot move furniture in until Oct. 15.

- **Business risk:** October is one of our busiest months for sales calls and we cannot afford to lose any.

- **Background:** the telephone company messed us around the last time we moved.

- **Technology:** we will take the opportunity to install a new state-of-the-art computer network for all administration.

Strategy

What must we do to take this information into account when planning *Project 1?* Some suggestions include:

- Sales Dept. must be the top priority; they should be moved first.

- Yes, install the new network wiring and so on, but let's settle in with the old systems; we can finish the network job after the move (i.e. a two phase approach).

- We should investigate using alternative phones (for example, mobile phones) as backups during the difficult period (contingency).

This powerful principle of asking the questions and acting upon the facts, increases the chances of success. From these answers, the details emerge. So, the outline sets of phases for *Project 1* could look like this:

1. Basic decoration

2. Install network and other wiring

3. Set up contingency sales dept.

4. Move In

5. Install new network system

What is emerging is the general outline of a plan for the project. At this stage, this level of detail is sufficient. Sometimes you must resist very strongly the temptation to dive too deeply into detail.

Documenting the project

You do need to write this down in some form. You will be questioned about the project and you should be very sure of your ground before initiating any project tasks.

Project definition

This is the time to introduce form SP1– the SP Project Definition Form. **In most cases, this will be the only formal documentation necessary for a small project.** On occasions where a project may need slightly more documentation, then extensions to SP1 can be used. As you progress through this book, following the stages of setting up and executing a project, the relevant parts of SP1 will be completed. Right now, at the project initiation stage, begin the process of writing down what you believe the project is, and how you intend to tackle it. This all fits on SP1. A complete set of blank forms is included in Appendix A.

First, the easy bits. Fill in the project name and brief description This may be a snappy name that people will remember and help easily identify the project. You can then fill in the sections based upon answers to the Strategic Factors questions.

Objectives

The Objectives of the project should be entered before anything else. They describe what it is all about. Also, priorities may come into play and this is where we can state them. Objectives should be SMART:

S   Stated Clearly, so there is no argument

M   Measurable, so you know when to stop

A   Agreed, by all parties, in advance

R   Realistic, and prioritised

T   Time-related, to give time targets

Here are some examples. The objectives of *Project 1 (Office Move)* could be:

- To move the entire contents of the office from Location A to Location B by Oct. 31.

- Not to lose a single Sales Enquiry while moving

- To install a new network system

- Installation of the new network is a lower priority than maintaining a full sales service.

Once the Objectives have been agreed and written on SP1, they form a base from which the project can be managed.

   If the objectives change during the course of the project then they can be re-visited, amended and re-agreed. Think of them as forming part of a contract between the

Project Sponsor and the Project Manager (don't worry about these terms, more about them in Chapter 3).

The Objectives are the underlying basis of the project; however, they can always be changed, with agreement.

Scope

The Scope of the project is the next item to document. Again, based upon the answers to the Strategic Factors questions, you can now specify what is included in the project, and almost more importantly, what is NOT included.

Scope describes parts of the organisation, geographical areas, branches of the business, or whatever. It's the scope that provides the boundary around the project.

- The *Project 1 (Office Move)* Scope might be: The move includes all office equipment, furniture, shelves, and staff, but excludes carpets, blinds, and the telephone system.

- The *Project 2 (Exhibition Stand)* Scope might be: The project must include the design and production of all exhibition give-aways, staff travel and accommodation, and a sales leads follow-up system, but it does not include buying the stand or any of the fittings, as these will be supplied by the Exhibition Organisers.

Defining the scope is essential. By establishing agreement to the scope at the initiation stage you can reduce the chance of disappointment at the end of the project when people don't get what they expected.

Again, an agreed scope at the outset gives you a base to return to if you discover that the scope needs changing; unmanaged creeping scope is the bane of all project managers.

Constraints

Next on the list are the constraints on the project. Traditionally, constraints include time (start dates, end dates, seasonal considerations), resources (availability and skill levels of people), budget, methods and rules that have to be followed, and so on. The constraints for *Project 1 (Office Move)* might include:

- We must be out of the old office by Oct. 31.

- We cannot get into the new office until Oct. 1 and, even then, we cannot move furniture in until Oct. 15.

- October is the busy season for sales

The constraints for *Project 2 (Exhibition Stand)* might include:

- Give-aways must be produced three days before exhibition, for shipping

- The budget limit is $1,500

- All give-aways must conform to the new corporate image standards

Documenting constraints is vital but must never be allowed to turn into a back-covering exercise. The project cannot be planned or managed without a clear statement of the constraints. If the project has to change shape later during its life the constraints may need to be reviewed (for example, a date might be relaxed, or more money found to overcome a problem). Without the initial agreement on constraints, all subsequent actions can be rather reactive, with no mechanism for understanding the consequences of changing a constraint.

Roles and responsibilities

This section deserves its own chapter and is dealt with next.

Main products/deliverables

At this stage it is also important to establish and agree exactly what is to be produced by the project and, where necessary, agree on the format.

All projects produce something tangible, and the Main Products/Deliverables section on SP1 is the place to state what the project is designed to produce. The end product (many people use the term deliverable; the terms are interchangeable) and, to some extent, the intermediate products can often be a source of confusion and misunderstanding. So the better they can be defined at the outset the more chance of success.

Many projects produce 'only' a report; state what the report is to be used for and, if known at this stage, list the major topics to be covered by the report. The principle behind this section of SP1 is to avoid the surprise at the end of the project, when the sponsor gets something they didn't expect.

If there are company or legal standards to be followed, this can be stated here to clarify the nature of the product. If the product is to be the subject of a series of stringent quality checks, these can be spelt out in more detail on the Project Quality Plan form, which is described in Chapter 8.

An example for *Project 1 (Office Move)* might include a technical specification of the new network, including performance and resilience characteristics. This definition will give the technical members of the project team a clear target at which to aim.

External dependencies

The section to complete at this stage also uses information straight out of the strategic factors questions. Very few projects nowadays take place in isolation; most organisations have several (even many) projects under way at any one time. In many cases these projects interact with each other.

The external dependencies section of SP1 is the place where you can take note of the way that other projects will influence your project. Such information is vital in the planning process. For example, the external influences section for *Project 1 (Office Move)* might include:

> There is a company project looking into the new health and safety regulations as they apply to users of computers.

The external influences section for *Project 2 (Exhibition Stand)* might include:

The annual company conference is taking place the previous week. All publishing and graphics staff are fully allocated to preparing materials for that event.

External Influences for *Project 3 (New Mailing Database)* might include:

The boss has just initiated a project to look at buying name and address lists from third parties, and these might need to be incorporated into our future name and address system.

Assumptions

It is often impossible to bring all the project characteristics out into the open. Sometimes, because of a lack of time, or knowledge, you have to guess the key factors. There is nothing wrong with guessing, as long as two other precautions are taken.

First, write down the guesses in the underlying assumptions section of SP1. This at least shows that they are assumptions, not facts.

Second, put some actions into play that are designed to clear up the assumptions at the earliest opportunity. These actions may form an early phase of the project (many engineering prototypes are built in order to clear up assumptions about the end product). Then reshape the project based upon the information you glean from these actions.

Managing Smaller Projects: A Practical Guide

Phases/Tasks

Based upon the structuring exercise, the Phases can be
documented. If the project is really small then the Phases list
may be all that is needed. Usually, however, a slightly more
detailed project plan is required (more of this in Chapter 4). In
this latter case, the Phase list from SP1 becomes essential input
to the planning process in which the phase can be broken down
into more detailed tasks.

For very small projects, however, the Phase list is
enough. Just put down the phase names at present. Resources
and dates will be filled in later.

Outline Plan

As a result of asking the Strategic Factors questions and then
taking a critical look at the answers, you will know quite a bit
more about the project. You can see what it consists of, what
the objectives are and the major constraints. You also have an
outline plan (for that is what the Phase list is) showing how you
intend to tackle the project.

You have also started the process of documenting the
project in a simple manner, using SP1, the project definition
form.

There are several more sections of this form that must
be completed at the Project Initiation stage. The next is roles
and responsibilities.

42

Roles and Responsibilities

I t is important to get a clear definition of certain key roles in a project, and there is a simple approach to the question: 'Who is responsible for this?'

Jobs versus roles

A common approach to managing projects – especially smaller projects – is to appoint a skilled and experienced person to the ROLE of project manager. Often this appointment lasts only for the duration of the project. At the completion of the project, the person returns to his or her previous duties.

It might not be ideal, but very often the role is part-time, with the project manager having to achieve project objectives while holding down a routine job within the organisation.

It is also common nowadays for the project manager not to be the line manager of the project team. In fact, the project team itself may be a disparate mix of skilled individuals put together for the duration of the project.

None of these combinations matter much, as long as the roles and responsibilities are defined and understood at the outset.

Three main roles need to be given on SP1, the project definition form. The roles are 'Project Customer,' 'Project Sponsor,' and 'Project Manager.' Not every project will require people to be assigned to all three.

Finding the customer

The person who asked you to undertake the project may also be the person who will use and benefit from the end product (the thing that the project produces). It is more common, however, to find that the 'customer' is not the person who assigned you the project. This introduces the possibility of a divergence of views between the person who commissioned the project and the final user. For example, the Marketing Director, who initiated the exhibition stand project, may have a different vision from the senior sales person who will run the stand. Get the roles and responsibilities out into the open at the start (instead of at the exhibition!) as this will nip problems in the bud.

The term used to describe the person who benefits from the project is the 'Project Customer'. There may be a large number of apparent customers, but there is usually one representative who can be called the 'Customer'.

Examples

For example, the Project Customer for *Project 1 (Office Move)* is the supervisor of the office being moved. This is the person who will benefit from the move and will have to use the new setup.

The Project Customer of *Project 2 (Exhibition Stand)* is the senior sales person who will be running the stand.

The Project Customer of *Project 3 (New Mailing Database)* is the section leader who is responsible for maintaining the name and address database.

Why do we need one?

It is important to identify the customer for the following reasons:

- It is the Customer who will use the end product, so it ought to be the Customer who has a major input to the scope, objectives, and constraints.

- Most projects require the active support and commitment of the Customer for the whole duration of the project to have any chance of success.

The Customer's views and judgement will be vital if project priorities need to be reviewed and changed. Any arbitrary change to the main project aims made by the project team, with no reference to the customer, will whittle away at the customer's commitment to the project.

The Customer may be required to supply key resources to the project, albeit only part-time. These resources will probably also have to carry out their regular duties while helping on the project, so commitment to the project by all concerned is essential.

Early identification and involvement of the Customer is valuable. However, just pointing the finger at someone and saying 'congratulations, you are the Project Customer' is not enough! If you cannot tell them what their role is expected to be, then you do not deserve their support. So, think about the likely elements in the role of a Project Customer:

- Providing advice and input to the initiation stage, when Objectives, Scope, and Constraints are agreed

- Providing skilled and experienced resources to assist the project teams

- Contributing to decision-making concerning project progress, rescheduling etc.

- Informing the project team of quality issues, changing business requirements etc.

- Testing, or trying out, things produced by the project team, and advising on their acceptability

- Accepting the final end product

It is unlikely that the Customer's role will be full time, although it may well extend over the duration of the project. The Project Manager, when negotiating with the Project Customer's commitment, must be prepared to indicate just how much involvement will be needed and its timing. This can best be confirmed when the project plan begins to emerge.

The other important aspect of this role is that of authority. A small, quick moving project should not be held up because the Project Customer's representative does not have the authority to approve a key project item. Again, when the plan has emerged in more detail the scope and nature of the necessary authority can be identified.

The project sponsor

The concept of a Project Sponsor is commonplace, but many people, Sponsors included, have no formal knowledge of the role and its attendant responsibilities. This can lead to sponsors laying down the law about 'their project' with no idea of the consequences, or implications, of their actions.

As the Sponsor's role is so important, you must make sure that you understand why one is needed and for what the Sponsor should be responsible.

The Sponsor is one of the main decision-makers on the project. He or she is the 'champion' of the project when decisions about the project's interface with the business environment must be made. For example, if the project starts to slip against budget, the sponsor may have to go 'into battle' to obtain approval for more expenditure.

47

Examples

Likely Sponsors for our sample projects might be:

- *Project 1 (Office Move)*: Premises Manager

- *Project 2 (Exhibition Stand)*: Marketing Director

- *Project 3 (New Mailing Database)*: Marketing Director

You can see from these limited examples that senior management can collect many project sponsorships. They may find the idea of being a Project Sponsor quite attractive if they are unaware of the detailed responsibilities. It is very important to spell out the role of Sponsor before you ask someone to take it on. They have to realise that this is more than a figurehead role.

The role of the project sponsor

The detailed responsibilities of a Project Sponsor include:

- To approve the project plans (and by this I mean all aspects of project initiation)

- To agree and deliver necessary resources

- To monitor progress via the Project Manager

- To ensure quality via the Project Customer

- To resolve project-business conflicts (especially in the areas of budget and resources)

It is clear from this list that the role of Project Sponsor is not full time, but may involve intense activity from time to time. A prospective sponsor must understand this commitment before agreeing to take on the role.

In many instances, the Sponsor does not 'take on' the role, because the Sponsor is the initiator of the project. However, even in these cases, it is important for the Sponsor to understand the responsibilities associated with 'dishing out' a project. It is all too easy to feel very dynamic when you cause lots of people to scamper about while forgetting that responsibility is two-sided. When a project begins to run into trouble, the Project Sponsor has a key role to play in steering it back on course. This may be time-consuming and full of hassle; but it will be a major factor in the eventual successful outcome of the project.

The project manager

In its simplest form the responsibility of the Project Manager is to ensure that the project is successful. This means producing the required end products to the required quality standard, within the specified constraints of time and cost.

Why do we need one?

If the project team knows what to do, why do we need a Project Manager? Well, how did the team come into being, and how do they all know what to do? Who told them? Who will keep the project rolling along even when the world outside the project is changing rapidly? Who will the Sponsor seek out for progress information?

Some organisations run on democratic lines, with no 'boss.' This can work well, but a project can cut across different areas of responsibility. It requires a single point of reference. One clearly identified Project Manager, to whom all day to day decisions can be referred (in whatever democratic manner best suits the particular environment), will mean one centre of responsibility. Shared responsibility usually becomes no responsibility at all.

Where does the project manager come from?

Often the Project Manager will be appointed from the customer area. Such a person may have skill or experience that will be useful to the project team. However, too much technical interest can generate problems. There may be times when the Project Manager needs to stand back from the detail in order to make business evaluations and decisions. As long as the detailed responsibilities are understood and accepted, the source of the Project Manager does not matter.

Examples

The Project Managers appropriate for our example projects might be:

- *Project 1 (Office Move)*: the senior person in the office to be moved, or maybe a person from the Premises Dept?

- *Project 2 (Exhibition Stand)*: someone from Marketing?

- *Project 3 (New Mailing Database)*: someone from IT?

The last example is interesting because in many larger organisations the Project Manager is often appointed from the end-user community (i.e. the customer community), and not necessarily from IT. This demonstrates a swing away from technical specialists running projects to those with a business view. The selection and appointment of a Project Manager can have a major impact on the overall success of the project (see Strategic Project Factors), and is not something to be undertaken in a casual or offhand manner.

The Role of the project manager

The detailed role and responsibilities of the Project Manager should include:

- To identify project scope, objectives, and constraints, and to obtain agreement to them

- To plan the project at an appropriate level

- To monitor progress against the plan

- To ensure that appropriate quality work is being carried out

- To devise corrective actions for problems

- To inform and advise the Sponsor and the Customer of progress and potential problems

Just like the role of the Project Sponsor, the role of Project Manager cannot be taken lightly. It must be clearly understood and accepted by the proposed manager before the role is formally adopted.

To complicate matters further, it is very common for the Project Manager to be a resource (i.e. a member of the team) on the project. Indeed, it may be that the Project Manager is the ONLY resource available to the project. These situations make it even more important to get the detailed responsibilities sorted out before the project gets fully under way. We may be able to blame someone else later for not realising that they were supposed to do some work, but it doesn't help the project towards a successful conclusion. Indeed, if a project gets into the blame stage it has probably lost its main chance of success. All that is left is a mess which someone has to sort out.

Other roles

Some projects may involve other people with supporting roles. Examples might include:

- Auditors (internal or external)

- Health & Safety Inspectors

- Legal Advisers

- Personnel Specialists

- Specialists (e.g. telephone engineers)

These roles play more of a part during the planning of a project and will be dealt with later.

Combining roles

In many smaller projects it is not necessary to find separate people to play each of the three roles. It is common to combine roles so that, for example, one person may be both the Customer and Sponsor.

As long as the responsibilities of each individual are understood and accepted at the outset (they can always be reviewed later if necessary) and as long as all the likely needs of the project (in terms of authority, decision-making, communication, etc.) are covered, there is no harm in combining roles.

SP1, project definition

Once the people and the roles have been matched up, it is a good idea to document the arrangement. The form SP1 Project Definition, contains space to write the names of the Project Customer, Project Sponsor, and Project Manager. If you want to document the detailed responsibilities, then a separate sheet can be used.

Individual team members

It is not usual to produce detailed responsibilities for every individual member of the project team. However, in some circumstances, it might pay off. When someone is going to undertake a project task outside their normal job, then a short responsibility statement may be of assistance both to the Project Manager and the individual.

For example, on *Project 1 (Office Move)* you assign a junior office clerk the job of canvassing views on decorating and colour schemes, and then coming up with a proposal. This task would benefit from a simple note detailing responsibilities, especially in the budget area!

Summary

You must avoid the 'I thought you were going to do that' situation. You can take steps to define clear and accepted responsibilities at the project initiation stage by appointing a Project Customer, a Project Sponsor and a Project Manager.

The details of the individual roles may vary from one project to another. They may need to be reviewed and changed as a project unfolds, but as long as you begin with a defined start position you can cope with all sorts of changes and set-backs.

CHAPTER FOUR

Project Planning

M any people get hung up on the definition of a plan, saying that they don't have time to produce one. This probably means that they have the wrong idea about what a plan should look like. They assume that a plan needs to be a complex, graphical document, showing how every minute of every day will be used.

This misconception about the form and content of plans is particularly wrong for smaller projects. People sometimes say 'If I spend all my time planning then I won't be able to do the work!' How wrong they are.

What is a plan for?

Here are some of the questions that are often asked during a
project:

- Can it be done?

- Will it be finished on time?

- When do you need the printers to deliver it?

- The printers will deliver one week late – does this
  matter?

- I need to take Jenny away for something else. OK?

- How can we be sure that the end product will work?

- Can you also include...?

- The directors are visiting on Friday; what progress can
  you show them?

- How much will it cost?

None of these questions can be answered with confidence
without some sort of plan. Even if some of the 'variables' have
already been decided (for example, you've been told the end
date before you start!) there are so many variables to juggle that
some sort of written plan, however scribbled, is always better
than 'I've got it all in my head.'

More excuses

While we are on the subject, people put forward many reasons for not planning. Let's examine some of the more common ones:

- **As soon as I write it all down, it all changes:** Yes, of course it does, but it's not the act of writing it down that causes it to change; things change anyway. The value of having a written plan is that you can analyse and manage the impact of the changes.

- **It takes too long to plan:** This is only true if you are going about it the wrong way.

- **If I write it all down then I'm stuck with it; people will use it to hit me with if things go wrong:** How sad! A more positive viewpoint would emphasise the need to gain involvement and commitment from others by using a project plan.

- **I've got it all in my head:** Maybe, but can you also do 'What if's' in your head? What happens if you are ill?

If a plan has to be able to answer these questions what should it look like? A full blown, big time project plan would actually be a package of related documents, ranging from a full schedule (in the form of a Gantt Chart), through a critical path network, and on to a cost plan or budget. At the other end of the scale a small project may be perfectly well served by a simple task list. Other types of plan might include a wall planner, a diary, and so on.

Task	Resource	Jan	Feb	Mar	Apr	May	Jun	Jul	Aug
1. Task 1	Jim	■							
2. Second Task	Jenny	▪							
3. Another Task	Jenny	■							
4. And Now This	Jeff	▪							
5. The Next One	Jim, Jeff		■						
6. Task 6	Jenny		▪						
7. Nearly The Last	Jenny, Jim		■						
8. Penultimate	Jeff		■						
9. Final Task	Jenny		■						

Gantt Chart

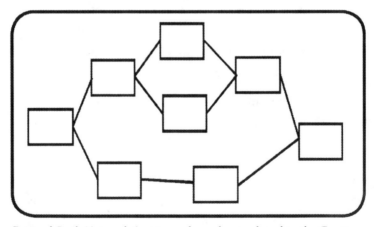

Critical Path Network (not to scale and not related to the Gantt Chart above)

```
┌─────────────────────────────────────────────┐
│         ┌───────────────────────┐           │
│         │   Project Task List   │           │
│         └───────────────────────┘           │
│  ┌─────────────────────────────────────────┐ │
│  │ Project Name and Brief Description       │ │
│  │                                          │ │
│  └─────────────────────────────────────────┘ │
```

	Project Tasks		
Phase/Task	Resources	Start Date	End
1. Task 1	Jim	Jan 03	Jan 05
2. Second Task	Jenny	Jan 03	Jan 05
3. Another Task	Jenny	Jan 06	Jan 15
4. And Now This	Jeff	Jan 16	Jan 21
5. The Next One	Jim, Jeff	Jan 23	Feb 03
6. Task 6	Jenny	Jan 23	Feb 03
7. Nearly The Last	Jenny, Jim	Feb 07	Feb 11
8. Penultimate	J Jeff	Feb 07	Feb 11

Project Phase/Task List SP6

For most smaller projects, a task list is enough, but we will identify ways of making it more useful by, for example, adding target dates, people's names, etc.

Physically, the task list could be hand written, typed, word processed, or on a flipchart, white board, or even Lego™ bricks! Whatever its format, the plan should have the following practical characteristics:

- Easy to amend (remember, it will change)

- Easy to read (for you and everyone else)

- Easy to distribute (if the project team need personal copies)

Finally, depending upon the particular project, the plan may also need the following characteristics:

- The ability to show costs/budgets

- The ability to show named resources (for example, People – Jim; Machines – mobile crane; Services – company lawyer)

The level of project plan we will focus on for SP is the task list, with resources, target dates, and costs. This is the minimum. There may be enhancements in the areas of risk management, quality management, change management, and multiple project management. These various extensions will be dealt with later.

How do I compile the plan?

Where the plan comes from is an interesting question. It is a great temptation for the Project Manager to compile the plan 'privately,' involving no other team members. This may seem like a good idea. The plan emerges quickly, with no interference, but a plan produced this way lacks width of vision.

Who can help you?

While the production of the plan must be a single person's responsibility, input to it must be collected from as wide a range of people as possible. The project manager should ask the following people for views as to what should appear in the plan:

- The project team
- Outside suppliers
- The Customer
- The Sponsor/boss
- Technical experts
- Legal?
- Quality experts
- Accountant?
- Other project managers

Where else can I go for help?

Various documents can provide sources of useful information at this stage.

- Previous project plans
- Company standards and guidelines
- Quality management system
- Technical manuals
- The project brief!

What should go into the plan?

The Project Manager should cast a wide net when gathering information to put in a project plan. There might even be a team 'brainstorm' to develop a draft plan. This can have the useful by-product of better project team commitment. Don't be afraid of leaving parts of the plan 'to be determined.' Knowing that there are unknowns is better than not knowing at all! It may be necessary to plan in some research tasks, designed to uncover more accurate detail for subsequent planning. Don't forget to include:

- All project work related to the project brief.

- Planning and replanning time. It's going to happen, so build it into the plan.

- Progress monitoring and reporting. This is especially required if you need to collect progress information from, say, an outside supplier.

- Team meetings.

- Quality reviews. A tricky one here is whether also to allow some 'rework time;' this depends upon your experience with QA in your organisation.

- Work done by outside resources. Ask the outside suppliers for a copy of their plan and see what sort of reply you get! Seriously, if they produce a plan they will probably produce the goods, and if not, watch out!

- Staff training. Especially training for any members of the project team.

- Time and tasks needed for the Project Customer to accept the end product.

- All external influences or dependencies should be registered in the plan, as they will be high on the list of potential problems later.

How big is a task?

The next question and a rather obvious one at this stage, is what should go in the plan? Just two task entries, 'Plan It' and 'Do It', are too high a level, while 200 entries, from 'Sharpen Pencil' to 'Staple Report', are too low level. A balance must be struck in the SP philosophy – you must not end up with clutter.

The final word on the detail of the plan should rest with the Project Manager. But here are some guidelines:

- No task should be more than two weeks long (else, too difficult to control).

- If a task involves a mixture of people, split it into several tasks (else, too difficult to control).

- If a task produces several different products, split it.

- If a task consists of 'activity, wait, activity', split it.

- If a task spans a major checkpoint (such as a progress meeting), split it just before the checkpoint.

- If a task produces a series of components that each require quality testing, split it.

- If a task contains a number of external influences (or dependencies)h split it, and allow some contingency for delays.

- If it makes sense to make one person accountable for a part of it, split it.

Project Task List

Project Name and Brief Description **Office Move**

Computers, Contents and People

Project Tasks

Phase/Task	Resource	Start	End	Status
1. Agree Decorations		07/09	15/09	
2. Document Current Network		07/09	15/09	
3. Identify Sales Contingency		07/09	15/09	
4. Decorate Offices		01/10	14/10	
5. Install Wiring		15/10	19/10	
6. Move Furniture		20/10	26/10	
7. Test New Network		27/10	28/10	
8. Move People		29/10	30/10	
9. Complete Sales Move		31/10	31/10	

Project 1

Project Task List

Project Name and Brief Description **Exhibition Stand**

Create and Run Exhibition Stand in York, April 10-12

Project Tasks

Phase/Task	Resource	Start	End	Status
1. Agree Theme		20/03	20/03	
2. Design Stand		21/03	23/03	
3. Order Stand Materials		24/03	01/04	
4. Design Giveaways		24/03	01/04	
5. Book Accommodation		01/04	04/04	
6. Produce Giveaways		01/04	04/04	
7. Brief Staff		05/04	05/04	
8. Attend Exhibition		10/04	12/04	
9. Post-Exhib. Review		17/04	17/04	

Project 2

As a very general guideline, tasks of two or three days in length are satisfactory. A 10 minute task may need separate mention if it is vital to the success of the project (such as a phone call to a supplier for a vital delivery date check). Of course, to do this splitting you must be fairly sure that you know how long each individual task will take. Task estimating is dealt with later.

We can begin to complete the Phases /Tasks List part of SP1 (or SP6 if there are more than 10 Tasks) now, so let us see some examples for our sample projects, opposite.

The importance of sequence

Just jotting the tasks down is fine. It already puts you ahead of many so-called Project Managers, but you ought to consider their sequence. Doing correct things in an incorrect order is a waste of effort. A plan for a larger project might try to express this sequence as a network, with a critical path calculated through the web of tasks.

You needn't go that far. A small project will probably have a smaller, simpler task list. Factors that influence sequence include:

- One task producing a component to feed into another task

- Chronological, or seasonal, or cyclical, sequence

- Simple geographical considerations

- Organisational factors (department A must be tackled before department B)

- Availability of resources (people, machines, etc.)

- Budget (we cannot afford to do it all at once, so we will do it in several pieces, one after the other)

- Availability of external inputs; we just have to wait for something or someone else

Resources (people, machines, etc.)

You cannot call the task list produced here an adequate plan without allocating resources to the tasks. Even if you think that, for example, you are the sole resource, you will often find that someone else is involved. For example, either the Project Customer or the Project Sponsor will be involved, usually at the outset and at the end.

Allocating people to tasks can be fraught with problems. It is no good thinking that it is now 'Fred's problem' just because you've allocated a tricky task to him. Remember who will be first in the firing line if the project fails – you, not him. So the matching of tasks to people must be carried out with care.

Resource availability

Such information must include:

- Does the person have the right skills for the task? If not, what allowance will you make? Will you build in training or coaching time (and who will do it, and do THEY have time to do it)? Will you live with slower progress because of lack of skills or failed quality checks caused by poor skills?

- Does the person have the right availability for the task? Are they fully available to your project (and what does 'fully' really mean), or are they part time (and how much part time)? Do you have any history of real availability from this person? Will they have to carry out their routine duties alongside the project tasks and who decides on priorities? What about simple things such as holidays and other commitments? Have YOU overcommitted them already (motivation through overwork is NOT recognised as a valid motivation strategy nowadays)? See below for more on this.

- Does the person have the right productivity for the task? Do they have appropriate tools, etc.? How motivated are they towards the project tasks?

Face up to it now

Some of these questions may take you into difficult areas. If you don't try to get answers now, it will be too late when the project starts to run into trouble. It might be that you know who you want, but they are not available. Replanning the project to take reality into account is far better than unrealistic planning based on 'with any luck.' It may be that if you can identify a shortfall of vital skills at the planning stage something can be done about it before the problem hits you.

Where does the time go?

Availability is such a can of worms that it must be tackled as a topic in its own right. People make classic mistakes in this area, such as assuming that someone is available to the project when, in reality, they are also occupied on their routine tasks. Factors to consider in identifying a person's availability for project work include:

A) How many hours per week do they work?

B) How many of those hours are spent on parts of their job that must continue alongside the project?

C) How many hours per week are spent on administration (timesheets, form filling, progress reports, signing other people's forms, weekly meetings)?

The real working week

The maximum number of hours available for project work is A-(B + C). You must then consider which other projects they may be involved in and their relative priorities. It may be that you will be lucky to get seven hours per week out of a key resource. It is better to know this at the beginning (and plan for it) rather than argue about poor performance later on.

Motivation?

Incidentally, there are several standard traps that many managers fall into. They believe that the number of available hours can be increased by isolating the person, cutting them off from all social contact with other people. This is a recipe for disaster. A normal amount of social contact per day is vital to keep people sane. Such managers also rely on overtime and long hours, not realising that many people will work long hours but, because productivity falls off, produce no more than they would have done in a normal working week.

The upshot of all this is that a piece of work that might take person A one full working day to complete might take person B two weeks, simply because of the availability of B. If these factors are understood at the planning stage they can be allowed for.

We can now enter the Resource names against the various tasks on our project plan, as follows:

Project Task List

Project Name and Brief Description **Office Move**

Computers, Contents and People

Project Tasks

Phase/Task	Resource	Start	End	Status
1. Agree Decorations	Jim	07/09	15/09	
2. Document Current Network	Jeff	07/09	15/09	
3. Identify Sales Contingency	Jenny	07/09	15/09	
4. Decorate Offices	Jim	01/10	14/10	
5. Install Wiring	Jim, Jeff	15/10	19/10	
6. Move Furniture	Jim	20/10	26/10	
7. Test New Network	Jenny, Jeff	27/10	28/10	
8. Move People	Jim, Jenny	29/10	30/10	
9. Complete Sales Move	Jenny	31/10	31/10	

Project 1

Project Task List

Project Name and Brief Description **Exhibition Stand**

Create and Run Exhibition Stand in York, April 10-12

Project Tasks

Phase/Task	Resource	Start	End	Status
1. Agree Theme	AJ, CKP	20/03	20/03	
2. Design Stand	CKP	21/03	23/03	
3. Order Stand Materials	CKP, Supps	24/03	01/04	
4. Design Giveaways	CKP, PR	24/03	01/04	
5. Book Accommodation	NL	01/04	04/04	
6. Produce Giveaways	PR	01/04	04/04	
7. Brief Staff	AJ, CKP	05/04	05/04	
8. Attend Exhibition	CKP, Sales	10/04	12/04	
9. Post-Exhib. Review	AJ, CKP	17/04	17/04	

Project 2

Nearly there?

So, the task list is looking good. It is a list of tasks with resources allocated, and target dates based upon the estimates of the amount of work and the person doing it. Costs can also be entered, as discussed in Chapter 5. You will have thought long and hard about the task list, especially in relation to the people assigned the various tasks. You have documented it all very nicely on SP1 or SP6, and the plan meets the various constraints of the project, such as end date, budget, etc.

Will it work?

Unfortunately, unless you can claim a direct link to a Divine Being, the project will almost certainly not turn out the way it is planned. It is not part of the role description of a project manager to be clairvoyant. Things may happen that are a surprise to the Project Manager and that jolt the plan. However, there are two things you can do to improve the chances of the project plan being successful.

One is the modern and sophisticated technique of Risk Management (considered in Chapter 6). The other is a scrappy and problem-laden technique called Contingency Planning.

One of the big unknowns in any project is 'How long will this take?' Some estimates are cast in iron. If a machine takes one hour to make one widget and we need 20 widgets, we can confidently plan for 20 machine hours, especially if we have a long history of making widgets. If we have to estimate how long it will take to reconnect the computers to the network once we've moved to the new office, we are on dodgy ground. Even the experts may not commit to a firm estimate.

Contingency allowance

Enter the scrappy and problem-laden technique called contingency planning. This is just about the most abused and misused technique in the project manager's toolkit. Many people approach the subject with dread saying, as they have said to me over the years: 'If I show a contingency allowance in my plan the boss immediately crosses it out.'

The problem in some cases is that we really do need contingency, but it is often the first thing to go when times get tough. I think that part of the reason for this is the way it is added to a project plan. Too many project managers work out their plans with some accuracy, then slap on 10% contingency and hope to get away with it. The whole point about contingency is that you should be able to justify it. A blanket 10% is unjustifiable so, of course, the boss will cross it off the plan.

A better way

A better way of incorporating contingency is as follows:

- Look at every single task in the plan. Ask yourself: 'Does this task need contingency?'

- The overwhelming number of tasks will not need any, but, for the few that might, ask yourself two more questions: 'How Much?' and 'Why?'

Write down your answers! These answers become essential working papers that support your project plan. If the boss says 'Why do you need all this contingency?' you can explain it, in detail.

We need the thought process

Now for the bad news. The boss may still cross it off the plan. You may think 'Well, what was the point of all that.' Think about it, you identified a dodgy task in your plan, which you are fairly sure will overrun its time allowance. You tried to manage the situation by providing contingency, but that method is not available to you. You must try something else, as the risk has not gone away. For more detail on what else to try see Chapter 6.

The good news is that the boss might appreciate the need for the detailed allowance and accept your plans. I suppose there might be a middle ground where the boss has a different view (or extra knowledge) concerning one of your problem areas. If you have written down your contingency proposals you both have something to discuss!

Summary

You now have a project plan that answers some pertinent questions about the project. You have identified the tasks that need to be executed, their time allowance, their sequence, and who will carry them out. You have considered the thorny question of Contingency and have documented the plan in a simple and clear manner.

You could now put the plan in the drawer, and assume that all will unfold just as anticipated. Better still, use the plan to increase the chances of a successful outcome. This is the theme of the next chapter.

CHAPTER FIVE

Estimating and Budgeting

The job of a Project Manager is simple! After all, there are only three variables in a project, and juggling three things is a relatively simple task.

The three variables are time, cost, and quality. Their interrelationship is often illustrated as a triangle, as seen on the next page.

Strategic project factors

Earlier we dealt with the Strategic Project Factors. This chapter focuses on using those factors to help estimate time and cost before starting work. Quality is dealt with later.

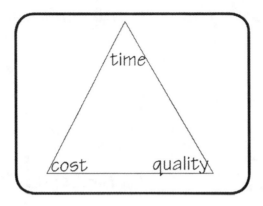

This triangle is dynamic: if you squeeze one factor you stretch the others.

Hold on, I hear you say, I already know the budget. My boss has told me exactly how much I can spend. He has also told me exactly when I must be finished. So why do I need to spend time on estimating time and cost?

Estimate versus given facts

Lucky you. Two of the most difficult things to establish have been stated right up front; see how easy this project management is! Seriously, just because someone has stated the budget and completion date it doesn't mean that you are off the estimating hook.

Questions to ask yourself include:

- Is the boss right?

- How did he reach these conclusions?

- When do we need to know he has been mistaken?

- How much leeway do we want if he is wrong?

The answers will vary. Maybe the completion date is immovable. Remember one of the underlying principles of good project management: you must realise that the boss could be right or wrong. Your job is to prove which is which and to offer suggestions and alternatives if the boss turns out to be mistaken.

So, even if the cost and time parameters are apparently fixed, you must still go through the estimating process either to reassure yourself that the job can be done within the given time and cost, or to identify possible problems and offer sensible alternatives. Let's begin by estimating time.

Staff hours versus elapsed time

Be sure that you know just what you mean by estimating time as there might be two types of time involved. If you are undertaking a fixed-price job then the number of staff hours involved is crucial; too many and the job loses money. If you are working to a fixed deadline then elapsed time is crucial, because if you miss the deadline you may incur penalties. Many projects have to take both staff hours and elapsed time into account. In this chapter we will look at estimating both these components of 'time.'

Do we need It?

You can simplify the task ahead of you by being clear about the need to estimate staff hours. If you don't need to know them, don't waste time on them. You only need to know staff hours if:

- You need an accurate Staff Cost figure, maybe for arriving at a price for the job.

- You are buying in some, if not all, the staff on an hourly basis and you need to know the cost.

- You are faced with very tight staff availability and you want to reassure yourself that the job can be handled.

- You have a wide range of staff grades involved on the project and you need to track various costs separately.

If none of these factors apply on this project you could jump straight to the task of estimating Elapsed Time.

This is an estimate!

You must remember at this stage of the project that you are producing an 'estimate,' not a fixed price for the job. Cost (and time) is an estimate or a fact; price is based on a corporate policy decision and need not concern us. However, if the price has been agreed, the estimates for cost (and the cost control mechanisms) become even more important, otherwise the job may lose money.

Let us begin by estimating the staff hours required to carry out the project work. You can see some overlap with Project Planning (Chapter 4) and to some extent the activities of planning and estimating run side by side. However, estimating has its own set of problems and concerns, so it is a topic to be tackled in its own right.

Which units?

Incidentally, I will use the term staff hours but on your project staff days, or even staff weeks, may be appropriate units. The staff hours are the hours of effort required to get a job done. The relationship between staff hours and elapsed time (i.e. how long it takes to do the job) is complex and is dealt with later.

There are two main inputs to this process. Obviously the task list is important, but so is the Underlying Assumptions section from SP1 Project Definition. There might be assumptions that have a major effect on the project. These must be kept in mind during the estimating process.

Estimating methods

Possible ways of estimating staff hours include:

- **Industry standards**: Guidelines may be available that tell you how many hours are required to accomplish a wide range of tasks, such as digging a trench, plastering a wall, writing program code, and so on.

- **Organisation standards**: Some organisations will have developed a set of standard times for certain well-defined activities. This makes the estimation of hours a simple arithmetic task.

- **Similar tasks**: For some jobs, we may be able to infer likely times from studying other, similar jobs.

- **Test measurement**: Do some work and measure it – sometimes called prototyping.

- **Ask the 'Worker'**: Find someone who may have personal experience of the job.

- **Suppliers' manuals**: These may give timings for using equipment, and so on.

- **Estimating software packages**: Quite common in a number of industries nowadays.

- **Your own experience**: Well, only if you keep reliable records.

- **Guess**: Nothing wrong with this, as a last resort, but back it up with test measurement at the earliest opportunity.

Time division?

Don't use simple time division. In other words, if you've got six hours to do three things, don't allow two hours for each one. It may be right, but it is usually wrong and painful.

You can note your estimates of staff hours against each task, in the Resource column, on form SP1 or SP6, whichever you are using for your phase/task list.

```
┌─────────────────────────────────────────┐
│        ┌───────────────────────┐         │
│        │   Project Task List   │         │
│        └───────────────────────┘         │
│                                           │
│  Project Name and Brief Description  Office Move │
│                                           │
│      Computers, Contents and People      │
└─────────────────────────────────────────┘
```

Phase/Task	Resource		Start	End	Status
1. Agree Decorations	Jim	12hrs			
2. Document Current Network	Jeff	4 hrs			
3. Identify Sales Contingency	Jenny	2 hrs			
4. Decorate Offices	Jim	48 hrs			
5. Install Wiring	Jim	8 hrs			
6. Move Furniture	Jim	8 hrs			
7. Test New Network	Jenny	2 hrs			
8. Move People	Jim	8 hrs			
9. Complete Sales Move	Jenny	8 hrs			

Elapsed time

Now consider estimating elapsed time (sometimes referred to as duration, business days, or working days). To create a more useful figure, write Start Date and End Date on the Task List on SP1 or SP6.

Do we need the detail?

For some tasks the job is very simple. You might be told by a supplier or sub-contractor that a particular task will take two weeks. If you are not interested in the detailed breakdown you can write two weeks against the elapsed time for the task.

Note that this could be made up of 400 staff hours for 20 people working flat out, or two staff hours plus a lot of waiting time, but if you are not concerned about the detail, two weeks is good enough.

Fixed length

For some tasks, the estimate can be considered as 'fixed.' For example, a trip to Birmingham to check out a supplier will take, say, one working day no matter whether one, two or three people go. Sure, the staff cost will vary, but the elapsed time remains as one day.

More people, less time!

Some tasks respond well to assigning many people. For example, to dig a trench 100m long may take one person 100 hours, or 10 people 10 hours. The staff time will be the same, but the elapsed time will fall.

More people, more time!

Don't get carried away, though, with the idea that throwing more people at a task will shorten its duration. Think of a progress meeting; more people means more time, not less!

The guidelines for estimating staff time can be applied to elapsed time, but bear in mind the temptation (or is it practical necessity?) to round up elapsed time into simple units (five Staff Hours for one person equals one elapsed day). This may be absolutely correct, but the relationship between staff hours and elapsed time is complex, and the elapsed time of every task must be considered carefully on its own merits.

Spurious accuracy

Never lose sight of the problem of 'spurious accuracy.' Who are we kidding if we say that a task will take 3.5 hours? Half a day amounts to the same thing and sounds much more sensible.

The exhibition stand project

Before going on to costs, let's summarise the job of estimating time. It is best seen by looking at the Task List of the Exhibition Stand Project (below).

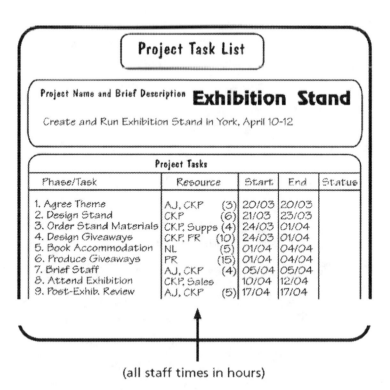

Project Task List

Project Name and Brief Description **Exhibition Stand**

Create and Run Exhibition Stand in York, April 10-12

Project Tasks

Phase/Task	Resource		Start	End	Status
1. Agree Theme	AJ, CKP	(3)	20/03	20/03	
2. Design Stand	CKP	(6)	21/03	23/03	
3. Order Stand Materials	CKP, Supps	(4)	24/03	01/04	
4. Design Giveaways	CKP, PR	(10)	24/03	01/04	
5. Book Accommodation	NL	(5)	01/04	04/04	
6. Produce Giveaways	PR	(15)	01/04	04/04	
7. Brief Staff	AJ, CKP	(4)	05/04	05/04	
8. Attend Exhibition	CKP, Sales		10/04	12/04	
9. Post-Exhib. Review	AJ, CKP	(5)	17/04	17/04	

(all staff times in hours)

Start date and end date

The use of Start date and End Date gives us real dates, allowing for weekends and holidays, that are much more practical for communication and control purposes.

External costs or all costs?

In producing a budget plan for the project you use form SP4 Project Budget Plan. This shows, for each relevant item, its cost against the day (or week or month) in which it is incurred.

The use of the term 'relevant item' is deliberate. For many projects it may be necessary only to plan and account for external costs such as goods and services (including human resources) purchased outside the company. Many organisations are perfectly happy with this type of budget, whereas some go a little further wanting to see the internal staff costs of the project included in the budget.

What are the elements?

Just as in estimating staff hours, you need to ask the question 'exactly what do you need to include in an estimate of staff cost?' Elements that must be considered (and maybe excluded from the project costs) include the following:

- Staff costs for the project team; or are they a simple company overhead?

- Staff costs of any assistance given by the end customer (or is that something for the customer to worry about?); this is especially tricky if the customer is an internal one (same organisation as ourselves).

- Purchases (and depreciation?)

The calculation of hourly rates is beyond the scope of this book, as is the apportionment of overhead costs.

Calculating staff cost has already been made easier by carrying out a detailed estimate of staff hours. Once the hourly or daily rates are known, the calculation of cost from hours is simple.

Other factors that contribute to the cost of a project include the following:

- **People**: Yes, all the staff hours we've talked about, but also recruitment, training, travelling, accommodation, expenses, and subsistence.

- **Equipment**: Purchase or rental of equipment needed to undertake the project; maintenance; and communications facilities.

- **Software**: Purchase or rental; maintenance; training; and installation.

- **Supplies**: Consumables (paper, etc.); cabinets, filing, desks; and tools.

- **Additional**: Office/working accommodation; storage; printing; and publicity.

In order to complete the project budget you need to be sure when the various costs will occur. Some will be one-off costs (for example, a purchase of equipment), some may recur during the project (say, travel and subsistence associated with work done at another office), and some may be continuous throughout the project (costs of temporary staff).

Form SP4 enables you to plan the costs in detail. Below is an example based upon the Exhibition Stand project.

SP4 Budget Plan for Project:

Budget Plan for Project: Exhibition Stand   page   of

		Item	23/03	30/03	06/04	13/04	20/04			
3.	a	Stand and lighting	120							
3.	b	literature racks	75							
5.	a	hotel deposit			200					
6.	a	brochure packs			500					
6.	b	pens with company logo			75					
6.	c	extra business cards				200				
8.	a	train tickets				60				
8.	b	delivery of materials				75				

The task numbers from the task list

Total the column to give a weekly budget

Total the row to give a task budget

CHAPTER SIX

Managing Risk

A nd now, with any luck...' or 'How was I to know that they would do that?' or 'If only I had thought of that earlier.' – it is sad, but many people adopt one of those positions at some stage during a project. Obviously, you cannot be clairvoyant. The job of project manager does not include the skills of seeing into the future, but all too often we leave things to luck when, in fact, there is a better way.

Things will still go wrong...

Risk Management is a simple but powerful technique. It is not totally foolproof in that things will still go wrong, but its use can seriously increase the chances of project success.

As with many topics in this guide, we need to start with a few definitions or, at least, a few simple descriptions of what I mean.

Project risk assessment

There is a range of Risk Assessment methods that are often used at the start of a project. These methods attempt to identify the risks involved in a project before the project starts and are often used during the feasibility study stage. They aim to highlight factors surrounding the project that militate against project success and prompt the Project Manager (and Sponsor) to change the basis of the project to lessen the risks.

This book is not concerned with such methods. Remember, we took the stance that the decision as to whether or not the project would start had already been made. We are focusing our efforts on making that project a success.

Plan risk management

So, I am going to look at a Risk Management technique that takes a project plan as its starting point. It attempts to make that plan more robust, more capable of dealing with the problems that life will throw at the project. The Risk Management exercise is the responsibility of the Project Manager, but as the outcome of such activity usually puts up the cost of the project, the Sponsor must be informed and consulted over intended Risk Management proposals.

During this chapter you will refer to SP1 Project Definition and SP2 Risk Management.

The exhibition stand risks

Just to make sure that you understand what I mean by risk, let us look at one of the example projects in a little more detail and jot down a list of some of the things that could go wrong with it. So, for the Exhibition Stand project, let's examine the project plan (Chapter 4) and list the possible problems:

- Stand design does not fit available space
- Stand design not liked by staff
- Stand materials arrive late
- Accommodation unavailable
- Giveaways too expensive
- Giveaways not ready in time
- Key staff not available to attend

Even in a simple project plan you can quickly write down a list of potential problems. If you were to call the project team together to add their views the list would be even longer!

But is it likely?

Of course, some risks are rather remote. I suppose a mathematician could tell me the chances of a jumbo jet crashing onto my office while I am writing this book, but frankly I don't lie awake at night worrying about it.

Also some things may be possible, even likely, but their impact might be small; if my unreliable coffee machine breaks down again I shall be upset, but I shall carry on typing!

89

These two characteristics, the probability of something happening and its potential impact should it happen, are the two defining characteristics of any risk. It is these two characteristics that you must identify and evaluate in order to manage the risks in your project.

Four-stage approach

The technique of risk management has four main elements, as follows:

- Identification and assessment
- Prevention
- Containment
- Replanning

The technique is simple but very powerful, and we will look at it by using the example from above, the Exhibition Stand project.

Assessment

Having identified the things that could go wrong, you need to assess them, their probability and their impact. You can use a simple system of assessment. 'H' meaning High, 'M' for Medium, and 'L' for Low. Some people add K for Killer – there is a place for this, which I will illustrate later. You can evaluate the risks in a simple table (opposite): the column headed 'P' gives the rating for Probability, and the column headed 'I' a rating for Impact.

Focus

You can now focus on say, High probability/High impact risks. These, by definition, are likely to occur and will cause us problems.

	P	I
• Stand Design does not fit stand	L	H
• Stand Design not liked by staff	M	L
• Stand Materials arrive late	H	H
• Accommodation unavailable	L	H
• Giveaways too expensive	L	M
• Giveaways not ready in time	H	H
• Key staff not available to	L	H

Incidentally, the use of K for Killer is usually coupled with a Low Probability problem that has a Killer effect; such 'L' Probabilities will need very careful consideration.

Risk acceptance

This 'focus' concept is very important. In very few projects can you ever 'manage' all the risks. You might not have the money, time or knowledge to change the situation, so just accept the risk as being present and monitor it closely during the project. You may decide, in these cases, to build up the containment side (discussed later).

I'm not saying that it is safe to ignore the Medium and Low risks. You may need to come back to them later, especially if they are coupled with Killer Impact, but you can begin with risk management of High Probability /High Impact events.

Prevention

The second stage of risk management – prevention, aims to reduce the probability of the risky event happening. Look at each H/H event and try to identify ways in which the probability could be reduced.

You can then build those activities (which, in risk terms, are called preventative activities) into the project plan. For example, for the Exhibition Stand project we could reduce the probability of the stand materials arriving late by using only standard fittings from our suppliers catalogue, by warning the supplier of the tight timescale or by reusing materials left from last year, etc.

Note that arranging a second supplier does not prevent the first supplier from late delivery; this is really a containment or contingency activity as you will only use the second supplier if the first one lets you down.

It has a cost

Preventative activities will definitely be carried out, so they probably raise the cost of the project. They need resources and may need to be slotted into a particular place in the plan. The unfortunate thing about them is that, with few exceptions, no matter how many such activities you put into your plan, it will be impossible to bring the probability of a risk down to zero.

Containment, or contingency

The third stage of risk management will be more familiar to many of you, it is concerned with contingency planning. Having done your best to prevent the risk from happening, you must now take the rather pessimistic step of assuming that the problem has occurred and ask yourself: 'What would we like to have had in place in order to reduce the impact of the problem?'

The answer to this question may be a series of activities that should be carried out. They are called 'Contingent' or 'Containment' activities.

Examples of containment activities for the 'Stand Materials Arrive Late' risk in the Exhibition Stand project are:

- Use last year's stand

- Hire a basic stand from organisers

- Order from second supplier

Test the contingency plan!

Containment activities are significantly different from preventative activities. The hope is that they are never needed so you shouldn't clutter up the plan with them. However, you may need to test them out, just in case you need them. It would look daft if the much-vaunted contingency plan didn't work! In the Exhibition Stand example it might be time to get last year's stand out of the basement and see what condition it is in before it is pressed into service.

If they don't clutter up the main plan, where do we keep them and what links them back into the main plan? This takes us to the fourth and final stage of risk management: replanning.

Replanning with triggers

Containment activities may lurk on a subsidiary plan. (The back of another envelope?) But the main plan may need 'trigger activities' built in. These trigger the appropriate containment action as soon as the problem is detected. The name trigger activity may sound very grand, but triggers are usually activities such as progress meetings (especially with a supplier), a quality check or the test run of something. In short, triggers are actions which you were probably going to carry out anyway in order to establish some facts, but now they have this other vital use.

SP1 Project Definition			
	reqd?		reqd?
Risk Assessment		Project Quality Plan	
Change Management Sheet		Project Budget	

Who should carry out risk management?

The responsibility for compiling a separate Risk Management plan belongs to the Project Manager. However, it would be a good idea to involve the whole project team in identifying risks and their preventative and containment activities. Very often the author of a plan can be blind to the risks it contains. If there is no project team, try giving your draft project plan to that nit-picking, critical soul found in every organisation. You may get back some useful comments concerning risky elements!

Form SP1 Project Definition, (opposite) is the form on which the project manager can establish and agree whether a separate Risk Assessment is required.

SP2

If we assume that a Project Risk Assessment is required, then the project manager can apply the four-stage approach outlined above, and record the proposed Risk Management activities on SP2 Project Risk Assessment (see next page).

There is space on SP2 for five separate risks. If there are more, simply use more forms – or change the project as it is obviously very risky!

There will be risks for which no prevention can be identified (such as bad weather); for these you must have plenty of Contingent Activities.

SP2 Project Risk Assessment

Risk:

Preventive Actions:

Contingent Actions:

Trigger Actions:

Summary

Remember the old adage; an ounce of prevention is worth a pound of cure. This is a good practical guide for Risk Management.

Preventative Actions stop problems occurring, and this must be a worthwhile project management activity.

CHAPTER SEVEN

Controlling the Project

P roject Managers adopt a variety of strategies when it comes to managing an in-progress project:

- Look, just get on and do it (abdication)

- That last task you just completed was $8 over budget (obsession with detail)

- The plans were excellent; what could possibly go wrong? (blind ignorance; lack of imagination)

- You'll have to work harder to make up lost time (desperation)

- I told them what had to be done; I expect them to do it and heaven help them if they let me down (persecution)

Retreat into 'work'

Statements, similar to those above, are usually made just as the project really starts to go wrong. Even these strategies are better than those of Project Managers who have no idea of the status of their project and who hide behind project 'technical activity' for instance, instead of carrying out some simple project control.

A small project will not require or justify a draconian, overbearing or bureaucratic form of control. So:

- Endless meetings   – are out

- Heavy progress reports – are out

- Simple checklists   – are in

Face up to reality

The simple checklist which forms the backbone of SP project control is based on a simple philosophy; project control should help us to FACE UP to reality. Here is the checklist:

F   Facts about progress

A   Assurance about quality

C   Confirmation about costs

E   Early warning of potential problems

U   Update the Plan

P   Publish the Plan

Facts about progress

How do you measure progress at the moment? Do you simply ask project team members: 'How is it going?' They reply 'Fine,' and you delude yourself by thinking that the project is on track?

They will not necessarily be lying but team members are human beings. They will be:

- **Optimistic** – we think we can get it done in time

- **Ignorant** – we're not even sure what we have to complete and by when

- **Members of a go-for-it culture** – we want to give it our best shot and not let anybody down

- **Afraid of the boss**

- **Unschooled in project management** – we feel that we might be running a bit late, but we won't bother the Project Manager with our problems

. . . we don't always give or receive facts.

Let me say, though, that I am not obsessed with facts to the exclusion of everything else. The manner in which people tell you things can be as important as the actual progress report.

Non-verbal communication

For instance, if you ask someone 'How is it going?' They say 'Fine,' but appear to be about to burst into tears it is clearly not fine!

Trembling and non-verbal communication will normally tell you a lot. There is still a place for sensitivity and interpersonal skills, even on a small project.

Back to facts. How can you collect irrefutable facts about progress? Don't attempt it by asking 'How is it going?' You will learn something, but it won't be factual. Do it by asking to see completed deliverables or products. Examples include completed reports, printed publicity material and a completed exhibition stand.

Exercise a little sensitivity over how you ask the questions, but be adamant in your own mind that a completed deliverable means DONE and an incomplete deliverable means NOT DONE.

Sensitivity

The same question can be asked in different ways. There's the demand: *You should have finished that, let me see it now.* Then there's the request : *You should have finished that by now, let me see it.* Its all in the intonation, enthusiasm, interest and other positive good vibes that you can get into your voice and manner. Show them that you are interested in what they have produced and they will be proud to show you. Drag it out of them, and they will be reluctant to show you.

Why do I put so much emphasis on completed deliverables?

- A deliverable can be tested, checked, weighed, measured or whatever; in short, its quality against a specification can be proven. Work done on time, on budget, but below spec. is a real problem to the project manager, as it probably has to be done again. Deliverables are measurable proof of progress.

- Completed means completed; it is the easiest check of all. The project manager does not want to be told 'It is 80% complete.' This is useless and dangerous information.

- Complete = complete = no more managing.
  Not complete = not complete = needs more managing.

Confirmation of costs

As each piece of work is completed you can calculate the actual cost. It may have taken much more time than originally planned to arrive at a specific milestone on the project. This will probably mean that the costs are over-running. This must be identified and the implications for future costs established. This is covered in more detail later.

Early warning of potential problems

It is all very well trying to understand where the project is at present. However, project management is also concerned with *acting* on present information to *alter* and *control* future events. What this means is that the project manager must learn to interpret control facts and identify their implications.

Only one week late?

For example, the project manager discovers that one of the key personnel suffered a sporting injury that kept him off work for one week. The sportsman is now back at work, fully recovered.

- Fact: one week lost on particular tasks

- Implication: not great, probably no further loss of staff effort

Further delays to come

But here is another example: the project manager realises that one of the key team members is not as skilled in an important area as was hoped.

- Fact: a particular task took twice as long as planned

- Implication: maybe all future tasks assigned that this person will also take twice as long as planned

These two simple examples show the importance of extending from facts into implications for potential problems. As a project manager you are not expected to be clairvoyant; you are allowed to be surprised by something (such as Jim Smith can lay carpet tiles at only half the speed of Harry Brown). However, you are expected to learn from your project progress so you are not surprised by the same things twice (Oh look, Jim is still taking twice the time as Harry).

So, the collection of facts about progress must also feed into the early warning of potential problems.

Back to the project definition

Another useful piece of input to this early warning process is the project definition, especially the underlying assumptions section. If the project manager discovers that one of the assumptions is invalid, then this might have a ripple effect down through the project. Remember FACE UP; it really is the project manager's responsibility to face up to the reality of the project. Work out the full bad news position (or good news, of course) and take or recommend the appropriate corrective action.

Before talking about the UP part of the control acronym FACE UP, there are a few practical details about progress that need to be considered.

Better progress meetings

With a focus on deliverables firmly to the fore, you can see that a progress meeting, for instance, changes from a recital of percentages of progress to a display or 'examination and acceptance' of a range of completed deliverables.

Such a reliance on completed deliverables is absolutely essential when the people doing the work are not under the direct line management control of the project manager. For example, if the work is being carried out by outside contractors, getting hold of facts about progress can only be achieved by the examination of completed deliverables: a decorated office, a tested wiring system, a set of skilled and trained users of a computer system.

Control takes time

There are several implications to this approach. One is that project control takes time (but what is the alternative?). The other is that project control should be linked to events on the plan that produce testable deliverables and not linked to simple events such as the end of the month.

Meetings linked to events

In other words regular weekly or monthly progress meetings may be useless if there are no significant deliverables to examine. Unfortunately, many bosses, Sponsors, etc. like to have regular progress reports or meetings because they think that is control. Maybe no-one has explained to them the benefits of another way.

A motivational factor

If it is tackled in a positive and supportive manner, then control via deliverables can be turned into a highly motivating, target-based project planning method. If the project manager can specify in advance what has to be produced and how it will be accepted, the person tasked with producing that product will stand a good chance of organising themselves to be successful.

The other side of this coin is that if the project manager cannot specify these things in advance, how can anyone be expected to do a good job?

Test it

A final point on how to collect facts. Don't be afraid to use old-fashioned techniques such as observation, measurement, tests and trials. For example, if someone is building you a computer system that is required to process 30 customer enquiries per hour, test it, time it and measure it under all appropriate conditions.

Back to our acronym: FACE UP. It should be obvious by now that FACE is about the collection of information and understanding what it means, UP (update the plan, publish the plan) is concerned with formulating and taking corrective actions. So, now let's look at UP.

Update the plan

Being realistic about it, the options open to a Project Manager faced with a replanning job are probably these:

*   **Scrap the project:** The Sponsor will need a lot of convincing about this; accurate plans and progress facts will be essential.

- **Extend the end-date**: If this is the only way out then it must be taken. Often, the Project Manager might have only one shot at this corrective measure, so the identification of a new target date ought to be accurate and binding. Quite a careful replanning operation may be needed in order to convince the powers that be that more time is needed.

- **Bring in more resources**: (people, machines, etc.) For this option to stand any chance of working, the Project Manager must know which type of extra resource (and when) would make the required difference. Just throwing more hands at a project that is in trouble will probably make things worse because of increased strain on the Project Manager.

- **Spend more money**: Someone is bound to ask How Much? Why? When? What For? The Project Manager must have answers ready in advance.

- **Reduce the size of the project**: The project manager could consider leaving out some of the work, either permanently or temporarily (we'll do these things in Phase 2). To make any sense out of this option, the Project Manager will need to have a clear understanding of the Sponsor's and/or Customer's view of the priorities. It will be no good proposing to cut out the vital elements of the project, leaving the Customer with a few inconsequential bits and pieces. Negotiation with the Customer is vital for this option.

- **Reduce the quality**: Do a poor job! Seriously, although conventional wisdom says one should never reduce quality, it is always worth thinking about. Maybe the original definitions of quality targets, quality products and so on were too optimistic. Perhaps the end Customer might accept lower quality in some areas in order to get the end product delivered on time.

To round off this section about Updating the Plan, let me summarise:

- Use your plan to confirm that your proposed corrective actions really stand a good chance of solving the problems.

- Use your plan to gain approval of your proposed corrective actions from the Sponsor. Often the Project Manager does not have the authority to implement the corrective actions. The usual route is for the Project Manager to recommend a course of action to the Sponsor, who then approves the recommendations.

Publish the plan

Whom do you need to tell that things have changed? Well, anybody affected by the changes. It is easy to overlook the fact that many of the resources involved in your project are probably involved in other projects as well. A slippage on one project might have a knock-on across a range of projects elsewhere.

Having said that the Project Manager should publish the amended plan as soon as possible, though there may be times when it is not necessary to be quite so quick. If the slippage is not great and if the Project Manager can get the project back on track before the next major checkpoint, and if there are no changes to resources outside the immediate project team, then maybe the plan can be updated but not published.

Generally speaking, though, on a small project there are no major intermediate checkpoints, just the end-date. The Project Manager probably has to publish!

In summary, Project Control helps us to FACE UP to reality:

F   Facts about progress

A   Assurance about quality

C   Confirmation about costs

E   Early warning of potential problems

U   Update the Plan

P   Publish the Plan

It may be painful, but the alternatives are worse.

CHAPTER EIGHT

Managing Quality

What is Quality? The basic answer is simple: Quality is what gives complete customer satisfaction, using the word 'customer' in the wider context of 'someone who receives something from us.' This is true for every kind of customer, whether internal or external. Some customer's needs will be sophisticated, others much less so, but all will judge the quality of what they receive by how their needs and expectations are satisfied.

There is no such thing as absolute quality, as it means different things to different people, depending on the circumstances.

Quality matters as much in services as in products, so let us try to define quality point by point. It can be a difficult thing to pin down. We all recognise it when we experience it, but how can it be put it into words?

British Standards Institute's definition

"Totality of features and characteristics of a product or service that bear on *its ability to satisfy a given need.*" What a mouthful!

A working definition

Basically, quality is giving the 'customers' what they want, at the right cost, on time, every time. In the fast food business, for instance, it might be fairly easy to specify the quality criteria for the process of serving customers. Indeed, for most processes that produce an end product or service, quality criteria can be devised fairly easily. But, what does 'quality' mean in the context of project management?

Taking the above definition, piece by piece, you can relate quality to project management.

Elements of quality

Giving the customer what he or she wants. But who is the 'customer?' The contractual customer of our product or service, or the user of that product or service? It may well be both. Quality means communicating with the customers of the project to ensure that their requirements are understood and agreed at the outset and that the end product will actually do the right job, effectively. Designing the product to meet customer requirements, using faultless procedures for, say, construction, reliable purchased services/components, skilled personnel, and so on.

At the right cost. Costs are related to quality expectations: a low cost can lead customers to expect a low quality product and a high cost to a high quality product. But they still expect that product to fulfil its specification and function. For example, a cheap paper cup will be expected to hold water just as well as an expensive china teacup. What customers are looking for in a quality product is value for money.

Costs can be related to the project. Most projects have budgets and one of the common problems of managing projects is budget overrun. It is no good giving the customer a high quality, high cost product if it's not what they want and it's going to break the bank and eventually the organisation. A Rolls Royce solution to a mini-car problem may be satisfying technically, but may be in the wrong league when it comes to costs.

On time. Timing is almost always a vital quality element of a service or product and can be another common cause of project problems. The 'perfect' service, set up too late to take advantage of a business opportunity will be a useless white elephant and a source of acrimony and embarrassment.

And more terminology

Two other well-known and poorly understood quality terms must be dealt with before we go much further. A clearer view of 'Quality Control' and 'Quality Assurance' will help you relate quality to project management.

111

Quality control

Let us take Quality Control first, as we all tend to know this one better. Quality Control consists of all the checks, inspections, reviews and monitoring activities carried out to ensure that the project is moving along correctly and that the service or product under construction is conforming to requirements (remember, the right thing, at the right cost, on time). These QC activities can take the shape of testing something to make sure that it works, trying out a set of operator's instructions to see if they are understandable and so on.

Quality assurance

Quality Assurance addresses the environment within which the project will take place, to make sure that everything is set up to contribute to a successful outcome. Most QA activity takes place before the project gets under way. The environmental factors to be considered are often expressed in six categories: People, Methods, Machines, Materials, Measurements and Environment.

- **People**: having the right people (skills, availability), carrying out the right jobs (plans)

- **Methods**: having predefined methods and procedures for carrying out the various tasks

- **Machines**: ensuring that you have the right machines and tools to carry out tasks effectively

- **Materials**: having the right materials, bought from quality suppliers, on time at the right price

- **Measurements**: measurements are needed to ensure a successful outcome

- **Environment**: environmental factors that could influence the success of the project and how they are managed

To put it another way, Quality Control is a reactive method of Quality Management (checking the work after it has been done) and Quality Assurance is proactive (building the right environment before the work starts).

Getting the QC/QA balance right

Too reactive a style of management can lead to high Quality Costs, because the work has been completed before the checks are made. Quality costs are made up of the quality control activities such as inspection, scrap and rework that come straight off the profit of the project.

There is also another hard message about QC, in that the further down the life of a project a problem is detected, the higher the costs of scrap and/or rework.

A well-known example of this effect was given by the Japanese copier company Ricoh, published in the *Times* in July 1993. Ricoh discovered that if a problem in the design of a new copier was not identified right away the cost of correction built up dramatically, as follows:

Phase in which Design Problem Found	Cost of Production (in US Dollars)
Design Stage	$ 368
Production Stage	$ 17,000
Shipment (i.e. at customer site)	$ 590,000

Such late identification of faults will also cause other problems – rescheduling, resourcing, recosting – all things that the customer may not pay for.

Quality should be 'built in' by effective assurance, not just 'inspected at' by careful control.

QC activities

Quality Control activities are:

- Controlling the project (measuring cost, people's time etc.)

- Testing sub-assemblies or parts of the end product

- Reviewing the end product upon completion

All these 'quality' activities are also core project management activities. As you can see, quality has a great deal to do with project management.

QA activities

So, let us now put Quality into a project context. Quality Assurance activities are:

- **Project initiation** - activities involved in getting the strategic factors out in the open before we start

- **Roles and responsibilities** - clear assignment and acceptance of personal roles and responsibilities

- **Project estimating and budgeting** - the people and money aspects

- Project planning - people, money and timescales

- **Managing the risks** - proactively

A project quality plan (PQP)

As part of project initiation activities, you must think about a plan for Quality. PQP is a proactive activity that sets up the environment in such a way that a successful outcome is more likely. This is an optional activity. Many small, low risk projects may not need a special quality plan whereas higher risk projects may benefit from one.

The decision on whether or not to create a separate PQP should be made by the sponsor, guided by the project manager. On smaller projects, for which no separate PQP is necessary, the elements of QA and QC that are still necessary are covered in sufficient detail inthe relevant chapters of this book.

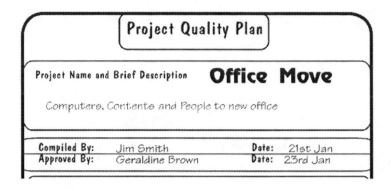

Project Quality Plan		
Project Name and Brief Description	**Office Move**	
Computers, Contents and People to new office		

Compiled By:	Jim Smith	Date:	21st Jan
Approved By:	Geraldine Brown	Date:	23rd Jan

SP5

The rest of this chapter focuses on how to write a PQP for a higher risk project. In documentation terms, we will use the standard form SP5 Project Quality Plan.

How to complete SP5 project quality plan

The first section is the standard project identification and brief description, and can be completed in accordance with the similar section in SP1 Project Definition.

Approved by

This PQP should usually be prepared by the Project Manager and approved by the Project Sponsor. The signatures of these key people record this fact.

Quality targets

These targets and criteria must be agreed upon and signed off at the beginning of the project, so as to avoid 'moving goal posts.' Of course, goalposts might have to move at times, but if you fix their position at the start, you are in a better position to judge the impact of their proposed move later.

The targets now become moments in time when certain predefined aspects of a project will be reviewed against predefined quality criteria, such as delivery date, development cost, and quality of product.

Delivery date and development cost can easily be specified and measured. 'Quality of Product' can be a rather nebulous phrase, so let us spend a few minutes describing how the quality of any product or service can be expressed. In fact, there are only five quality characteristics of any product or service, namely: *functionality, usability, reliability, performance* and *serviceability,* often referred to by the initials FURPS.

FURPS

FURPS can be best explained by example. Let us take a simple one first. You need to purchase a new washing machine and you realise that there are many models on the market. You can analyse and prioritise your requirements (i.e., your own quality requirements) with FURPS. Here is a set of FURPS for a new washing machine:

F Functionality - Well, I don't need any fancy washing programmes, just the standard range.

U Usability - I am experienced at using such machines and do not need a video screen control panel.

R Reliability - Top of my list; I need to use the machine every day and it must be reliable.

P Performance - It would be nice if it completed a full cycle within, say, two hours.

S Serviceability - Second on my list; if it breaks, I want it fixed at once .

The most important aspect of FURPS is the agreement that all interested parties must make to the relative rankings of the five characteristics. It's no good having the eventual end user of the product looking for one particular characteristic, say Usability, if the sponsor has decided that Functionality is the main criterion.

The beauty of a quality approach to a project is that discussions and arguments about the relative importance of these characteristics take place before any work or purchasing take place.

And now, the FURPS for our *Project 3 (New Mailing Database)*:

F Functionality - Yes; we have defined the functions we need, and they must be delivered.

U Usability - This is a major requirement, as the potential users of this new computer system have very little exposure to this type of system at present.

R Reliability - Being honest about it, this is not a system upon which the daily operation of the company depends; yes, it will be inconvenient if it fails, but we could continue our daily business.

P Performance - Not a big factor.

S Serviceability - We are concerned that we do not want to install a system that we cannot fix, maintain or enhance easily.

You can express FURPS on SP5 (see page 120).

This may include assessment against certain product standards, methods, technologies, and tools to be used during the project. If a decision is made to deviate from any normal practice, then the justification for that decision must be given. For example, you have an ISO 9000 Quality System in place and everyone agrees that as you will be building the system in-house you will dispense with the standard company procurement process for the mailing database project. As everyone has agreed to this and it has been documented, you can omit the standard procedure. Again, use SP5 (see page 121).

Project Quality Plan

Project Name & Brief Description **Mailing Database**

Name & address system for newsletter mailshot

Compiled By:	Jim Smith	**Date:**	21st Jan
Approved By:	Geraldine Brown	**Date:**	23rd Jan

Quality Targets:

1. Functionality as agreed in memo dated 10th Jan
2. Usability; most important: design for daily operation to be demonstrated before any programming work commences
3. System must be capable of easy alteration in future

Accepted By: Geraldine Brown   **Date:** 23rd Jan

Project Quality Plan

Project Name & Brief Description **Mailing Database**

Name & address system for newsletter mailshot

Compiled By:	Jim Smith	**Date:**	21st Jan
Approved By:	Geraldine Brown	**Date:**	23rd Jan

Approach to be used:

1. Standard Company Purchasing selection method not needed, as new equipment will be same as old
2. New Mailing Database must conform to (and be registered with) Data Protection Act.
3. New Database must use existing XYZ software, to facilitate easy maintenance

Implementation strategy

'How will you introduce the end product or service?' There may be no choice. You might have to implement the new service in a 'big bang.' An example from *Project 1 (Office Move)* is the way in which the service provided by the Sales Department must not be interrupted during the office move (see next page). If this is known and agreed up front then you stand a chance of achieving it; if not, not!

121

Project Quality Plan

Project Name and Brief Description **Office Move**

Computers, Contents and People to new office

Compiled By:	Jim Smith	**Date:**	21st Jan
Approved By:	Geraldine Brown	**Date:**	23rd Jan

Implementation Strategy:
Only 2 operators will be trained at first; 3 weeks pilot period, followed by evaluation of system, training & documentation, before roll-out to other 4 operators

Major products to be reviewed

This section enables you to decide which products (or parts of the service) will be reviewed and to document in advance how and when we will review them. Once the review has been carried out the findings can be recorded together with the actual review date.

If any corrective action is required to enable the product to pass review, this is agreed and recorded, together with who will carry out the corrective action and by when – the corrective action date. If the product requires a great deal of corrective action, this will incur Quality Costs and may have a detrimental effect on the rest of the project, in timing, costs and resources.

If SP5 is completed – after consultation between the sponsor, customer and project manager – then the project will start to unfurl in an environment that should lead to a successful outcome.

CHAPTER NINE

Managing Change

The two most common reasons for projects going adrift are an unclear or ill-defined definition (scope, objectives, or constraints) at the initiation stage, and poorly managed changes once the project has started.

If you go through the steps outlined in Project Initiation (Chapter 2), you should reduce the unclear start problems. This chapter focuses on managing project changes.

Change is inevitable

SP is a practical method. So, once a project definition has been signed, it is not possible to say that the project is frozen for life. It may be a source of constant frustration and aggravation to

the Project Manager to have to change the project, but life is
life and any project management approach worth its salt must
be able to cope within a changing environment. SP works on
the principle that change is inevitable. What you need is a way
of managing those changes and their impact on the project.

I have deliberately kept the approach very simple.
There are more sophisticated change management systems
available, but these are more appropriate for projects larger
than the SP guidelines.

Types of change

What types of changes are we talking about? Examples might
include:

- **Scope**. Requests to include new things, drop original
  items, or change the size of some items. For example,
  in the Office Move project: can you now also arrange
  for the old offices to be redecorated after we've moved
  out?

- **Objectives**. A change to the original aim. For example,
  in the name and address database project, the original
  objective of designing and building a new system is
  changed to carrying out a feasibility study and
  recommending a way forward.

- **Constraints**: time (we've got to bring it all forward
  three weeks); resources (I've got to take Jenny away to
  work on something more important); or budget (we
  can't spend any more in this financial year, but it is OK
  for next year).

- **Risk.** Changes usually entail increased risk, not decreased (we've got to use Dabit & Splashit as decorators, there is no choice).

Three stages

Managing changes to a project is a three-stage process:

- recognise the change as a change

- categorise it —— size
  ↘ priority

- process it —— action
  ↗ reject
  ↘ defer

Recognising the change

Sometimes a change comes through the door clearly labelled as 'Change.' This might be a statement from the boss, the sponsor, customer, or whoever, that they wish to change the project. Whether it is actually a change or not must be established. It might simply be that the person requesting the change has misunderstood (or has never seen) the original Project Definition (SP1).

Changes that sneak up

The majority of changes sneak up on the project manager, hidden within casual remarks, memos, other people's project progress reports and so on. The project manager must maintain a high level of vigilance in order to detect potential changes to the project.

To do this he or she must have the project definition always in mind, and must carefully check potential changes against the original, signed-off definition.

Baseline

The project definition is the baseline of the project, accepted by all relevant parties and the fixed point back to which all progress will be measured. It is therefore, together with any supplementary documents such as SP2 Risk Assessment, the essential input to the project manager's change management process.

Once the Project Manager has detected a change to the project basis, the temptation simply to accept is as a *fait accompli* must be avoided. There is a vital step in the process that must be carried out before any commitment can be made; namely, categorisation. Changes should be analysed in two ways: by priority and size.

Priority

- **Essential**. The end-product or service that is the subject of the project will be no good without this change (won't work, will be too late, will cost too much, etc.)

- **Useful**. This change will improve the end-product or service, but it is not essential.

- **Cosmetic**. Exactly what it says.

Size

- **Fundamental**. This change can only be incorporated by changing the fundamental parameters of the project; for example, the agreed end date may have to shift, or the budget will increase.

- **Tolerable**. The change can be incorporated within the current project parameters, maybe by consuming the Project Manager's contingency, or by cutting back or cutting out something else.

- **Trivial**. The change is of such limited impact that no significant replanning is required.

You may ask why it is worth bothering to analyse and document trivial and cosmetic changes? Well, there are two answers to that question:

1. **Trivial** - How does the Project Manager know that a change is trivial, without stopping to think about it? Often such changes are announced with a degree of ballyhoo that belies their impact on the project; they may be very important in the eyes of their proposer.

2. **A thousand cuts** - Two dozen trivial changes, poorly managed, can damage a project almost to the point of failure.

Limits of authority

So, having analysed and categorised the potential change, we can represent the various combinations in a table which illustrates another aspect of Change Management, namely Limits of Authority.

There are three levels of change to consider. The Project Manager's 'Limits of Authority' may be spelled out in the Roles and Responsibilities section of the Project Definition. Often it isn't spelled out, but is left to the judgment of the individual Project Manager.

Some guidelines

As a suggestion for steering the Project Manager into safer waters, a common approach to 'Limits of Authority' is to agree on guidelines such as these:

- Essential/fundamental, essential/tolerable, and essential/trivial changes must be incorporated, unless the Project Sponsor expressly rules against one.

- Useful/fundamental and useful/tolerable must be debated before action, rejection, or deferment.

- Cosmetic/fundamental, cosmetic/tolerable, cosmetic/trivial, and useful/trivial can all be rejected unless the Sponsor expressly selects one for action.

size / priority	fund'tal	tolerable	trivial
essential			
useful			
cosmetic			

Possible abuse

Now, you may have spotted the flaw in this little system of rules, the categorisation into priorities is open to abuse. The sizing of a change should not be an issue. The Project Manager, using the project definition and project plans, should be able to

131

justify any estimates of size; however, the establishment of priority should be the responsibility of the Customer or Sponsor. Herein lies the potential for abuse. How often have you seen 'top priority' attached to all changes making such prioritisation meaningless?

Sign-off

A meeting to discuss and agree on the priorities of changes – and agree potential changes to the schedule – will help in this 'top priority' situation.

SP has a tool to counteract this potential for abuse. Every proposed change must be signed off before it is actioned. This step may go some way towards damping down an over-enthusiastic proposer of changes.

Document the decision

The final step in Change Management is that of Process, which has three possible outcomes:

- **Action**: the change is accepted, signed off and will be incorporated.

- **Reject**: the change is refused.

- **Defer**: the change is accepted, but not to be actioned at present. The change may be incorporated in a later project, or in a later stage of this project.

SP 3

SP does not impose any form of documentation of Rejected or
Deferred changes, but suggests that changes that are accepted
for Action should be documented. SP3 is offered as a way of
doing it.

Example

Using the example of the Office Move project, the suggested
change of 'Redecorate the old office after the move' can be
added to SP3.

Change Management

Project Name and Brief Description   **Office Move**

Computers, Contents and People to new office

Compiled By: Jim Smith   **Date:** 21st Jan

Change: Redecorate Old Office after all staff and
equipment have been moved out

Implications: Not a lot; need to agree decorating scheme
with Dabit & Splashit before the move, then
let them get on with it

Accepted By: Geraldine Brown   **Date:** 27th Feb

The office move project

The form will be kept with the other project documents as it alters or qualifies some of the entries on the original Project Definition. As it is used throughout the project it will provide a history of changes.

In summary, change is inevitable even in a small project. SP hits the balance of low-overhead, practical control together with security and documented agreement.

CHAPTER TEN

Reviewing the Project

There comes a time on every project when someone says 'Are we going about *this* the *right way?'* You need to be absolutely clear about what I mean by this question. I don't mean 'Are we on track?' – a simple and valid project control question. I do mean 'Are we doing the right things from a project management point of view?'

The manner in which this question is answered can often have a major bearing on the future direction and success of the project. So you must spend a little time considering the question and a way of answering it that helps in making sensible and positive decisions about the project.

Let us take the initial question apart and focus on each component in turn:

- **Someone says:** Who is 'someone?'

- **A time on the project:** When could or should the question be asked?

- **This:** Is 'this' still valid (i.e. has the project changed out of recognition)?

- **Right way:** What is the right way? Who can ask this question?

Who cares?

Obviously, the Project Sponsor has rights in this area. Why should the sponsor pour good money after bad if the project is so badly run that the money will be wasted?

The Project Manager ought to be able to ask the question, even if it is asked privately. The project team ought to be able to ask the question, so that they feel that their efforts are being directed wisely. The Project Customer ought to be able to ask the question, to be reassured that the end product will be all that is required.

With so many people capable of asking the question, there must be a standard approach to this situation otherwise the Project Manager, who probably will have to provide the answer, will be swamped with a range and variety of time-wasting questions.

Now, let us consider the timing. When would someone ask the question 'are we. . ?'

When is a good time to do this?

There are several times in the life of a project when the
question should be asked:

- One of the most obvious occasions occurs when the
  project hits a large stopping point, maybe when
  something serious has gone wrong.

- Change the tense of the question and a constructive
  point at which to ask it comes after the project has
  been completed. This is the opportunity to learn how
  to improve and do it better next time.

- A subtle, but valuable, time to ask it happens when a
  new Project Manager has to take over, maybe because
  the previous Project Manager has been moved on to
  something else. The new manager needs to take stock
  of the situation very quickly, as people may be looking
  for fast action to sort something out.

- A good time to ask the question comes when it is
  realised that the original project scope, objectives or
  constraints have changed out of all recognition. A
  review of them is essential.

Lastly, we need to know what the 'right way' is in order to ask
'are we...' If you can define the 'right way' in a neutral and
constructive manner you stand a better chance of reviewing the
project against it and winning approval from all parties to any
changes.

Who is to blame?

In defining the 'right way' to manage a project and therefore a means of reviewing any project against the 'right way,' there must be a method of defining it that satisfies certain criteria:

- **Non-personal**: For any review to succeed, the project players must feel that the project is being reviewed, rather than them as people; roughly translated, this means that a project review must not turn into a witch-hunt or a search for someone to blame.

- **Checklist approach**: So that all aspects are considered.

- **Quick and simple to operate**: To encourage frequent use of the checklist; so that, if necessary, the Project Manager can carry out a review without stopping the whole project in its tracks or interviewing the entire project team one at a time.

So the SP project review method consists of a checklist that can be followed in a non-personal manner, producing a constructive review of the key elements of the project, that will either satisfy the concerned parties or bring about a series of positive changes to get the project back on track.

The outcome from such a review is either a formal report to the Project Sponsor or Customer or the Boss, or an informal report for the internal use of the Project Manager and the project team. Either way, the findings should be documented in some way so that they can be acted upon and not lost in the welter of project paperwork.

A formal 'Project Review Report' may sound rather imposing for a small project, yet it can be a very useful document. If you want to improve your performance as a project manager, you must carry out some project management work, measure what you do and then plan to improve it. A Project Review Report, however informal, can help us become better project managers.

So, here is the checklist. The report should be structured around this list, with a series of recommendations as the final statement:

Basis

- Was the purpose of the project clearly defined at the outset?
- Did everyone agree?
- Did it change as time passed by?
- Did the project have a business objective?
- Was the end product clearly defined early on?
- Were success criteria defined?

Plans

- Were there any plans?
- Was there a Project Definition (SP1)?
- Were the plans used or just forgotten?
- Were they realistic?
- Were deadlines, budgets, product targets met?

Personnel

- Were the right people available to work on the project, at times and quantities required?

- Was the team composed of the right skills and experience?

- Was the team productivity acceptable?

- Did the team members achieve job satisfaction on this project?

- Did the project enhance the team members reputation, skills, or development?

- Did the team members behave professionally?

Working methods

- Were appropriate and useful techniques, standards, etc. used?

- How useful were they?

- Were appropriate tools used?

- Were the facilities acceptable (accommodation, computer facilities, etc.)?

- Was the level of support satisfactory (training, guidance, clerical, etc)?

Project management

- Was there any project management carried out?

- Was the project manager sufficiently experienced, skilled, trained, and supported?

- Did the project manager have or make enough time to carry out the project management duties?

- Did the project manager have enough authority?

Control structure

- Were appropriate levels of control exercised?

- Were procedures for measuring progress, etc. devised and implemented?

- Was the control overhead justified?

- Did the project control activities support the team?

End product

- Do the customers use it?

- Did it fulfil its business objectives?

- Will it be as reliable, flexible, and maintainable, as required?

- Will it be cost effective?

So what?

For every one of the questions above, there is the subsidiary question 'So What?' It might be that there were problems with obtaining key people at the required time. Did it really make any difference to the project? If the answer is 'No', then you can merely document your findings; a recommendation for improvement may not be required.

If the answer is 'Yes', then you must devise some recommendations to improve the project management situation for next time.

What improvements can we make?

Recommendations for improvements may tackle the root cause of the problems, or simply point out that certain elements exist in the project management environment and must be endured or accepted.

For example, if a major problem is identified with the time taken by senior management to accept and sign-off the initial Project Definition, either learn to live with the situation – by changing people's expectations about how quickly projects can start – or recommend a change – such that the review and acceptance of Project Definitions becomes a regular feature in the weekly management meeting.

The SP improvement cycle

The whole reason for conducting a project review is to improve the way in which projects are managed, either the current project or all future projects. Improvement only happens through management action; management action only happens through the presentation of reasoned argument, backed up by facts and recommendations.

The SP approach to Project Review provides all these elements, and supports a simple self-improvement cycle.

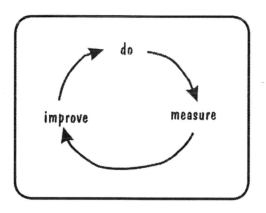

CHAPTER ELEVEN

Managing Several Projects

S o far, this book has taken you through the main elements of managing a small project (i.e. one small project). The overwhelming majority of readers will find themselves in the position of managing several (or many) projects at the same time. In fact, the common mix of responsibilities that form the workload of a typical project manager looks like this:

- **Projects**: a number of packages of work clearly labelled as 'projects.'

- **Staff management work**: recruitment, appraisals (both conducting and receiving), training planning, training delivery, informal coaching, counselling, discipline, and writing procedures, rules, and guidelines.

- **Reviewing other people's work**: either formally (in a Quality Review) or informally ('Just have a quick look at this, will you, before I send it out?')

- **Company business**: weekly/monthly management meetings, annual meetings, roadshows, or open days.

- **Company/social business**: sports and social events, or work experience schemes.

- **Social intercourse:** just talking to people, getting coffee, going to the washroom, fixing up a tennis match, etc.

- **Company administration**: filling in timesheets, progress reports, expenses, holiday requests, purchase orders, etc.

- **The routine job**: the project manager's 'own job,' whether it is sales manager, accounts clerk, warehouse manager, computer technician, etc. This job, of course, must be fulfilled without noticeable adverse impact.

Macho motivation

While we are on the subject of the balancing of demands of a routine (full-time?) job against the pressures of managing a project, let me state something with which many senior managers may disagree...

It is not motivating to pile a so-called career opportunity on top of a regular job. Macho motivation, applying multiple pressures to key staff members, is totally discredited as a motivational strategy. Yes, such pressure can get people moving, often through fear, but when the pressure is relaxed the people slow down. Movement caused by external pressure is not the same as, and not as effective as, motivation caused by internal drive.

The effective manager will find out what things motivate every one of the individuals who make up the team and provide those things; this is the only true way to motivate a team of individuals.

This is beginning to sound like a sermon and people management issues are beyond the scope of SP. However, the common effect of over-optimistic dumping of work (we cannot call it delegation, as that implies thoughtful management) is, among other things, a major cause of project failure and this is a legitimate concern of SP.

Returning to the analysis of the workload of a typical project manager, you can see that project work may take a very low priority at times. The interesting question to contemplate, and one posed in a different way in Chapter 4 (Project Planning) is: 'How much time will the project manager be able to devote to Project Management?'

How much time can YOU spare?

People approach this question in a variety of ways:

- **Ignore it** – take on too many commitments; wonder why they never get anything done.

- **Answer it too optimistically** – results as above.

- **Try to measure it** – the 'scientific' approach with, usually, frightening results.

147

Do you really know where your time goes?

Before taking on the challenge of managing a project alongside your normal work, a revealing first step is to measure where you spend your time. Try completing a timesheet for a few weeks. Summarise the results and discuss your findings with your boss. In any event, what you are trying to establish is where your time goes and therefore which jobs you might have to stop, or pass on to someone else, in order to take on some project management responsibilities.

Now, let us assume that you have measured and managed your time. The next question is 'How can you plan and control a multitude of jobs?'

Get the basics down first

Follow this sequence:

1. Write down all the fixed activities that you must carry out such as monthly management meetings, progress reports, etc.

2. Write down all the personnel management activities you must carry out that you cannot delegate such as the appraisal of immediate subordinates.

3. Write down all of your project activities.

Diary dates

One effective way of coordinating a whole bunch of smaller projects is to extract from each project definition the key project dates – when a task must be completed, when a quality review shold take place, when a risk trigger must be tested – and write them all into a diary.

Then, at a glance, you can see all of the project events due on a certain day. If you have already entered the fixed and unavoidable commitments into the diary, you will be able to identify commitment clashes (either for you or key staff members), the domino effect of one project delay across other projects, and so on.

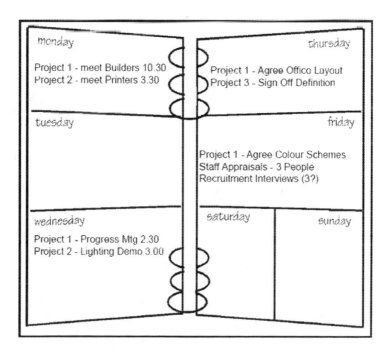

Using a Filofax

So, on the previous page is an example using a Filofax-style personal organiser as the 'consolidation' mechanism. There are three projects on the go this week, together with some line management tasks. Wednesday and Friday look particularly busy and could cause problems. The Project Manager should consider taking action as follows:

- delegate one of the two events on Wednesday, or reschedule if delegation is not an option

- delegate either the colour scheme job or the recruitment interview job

- deferring the staff appraisals should be resisted, as the staff concerned might not like to be lower in priority than agreeing to a colour scheme!

Using a wall planner

Another simple but effective way of consolidating a number of projects into one clear picture is to use a wall planner. Many people copy the wall planner onto paper (11x17 is a good size), which is usually more portable.

The same principles apply as before:

1. Write down all the fixed entries first (holidays, monthly management meetings, etc.).

2. Write down all the personnel management activities next (appraisals, recruitment, induction, training).

3. Now, write down significant dates and events selected from your portfolio of individual project definitions.

Problems of resource clashes, overloading of the Project
Manager, and so on should now begin to emerge.

1	2	3	4	5		
8	9	10	11	12		
15	16	17	18	19		
22	23	24	25	26		
29	30	31				

Challenge the priorities

Does it all fit into your time allowance? Can you do your
week's work within one week?

If the answer is Yes, excellent!

If the answer is No, then you must challenge and
reaffirm the relative priorities of project work versus other
work. With your plan, even if it is only a simple list of
commitments, you have something to take to the boss.

Monitor against your assumptions

Assuming that any problems are resolved, you now have a very important thing to do. You must monitor how your time is actually consumed (yes, even if it means the dreaded timesheet again).

Having taken all this trouble to base your future workload on some factual breakdown, it is vital that you verify the actual time consumption. Then, if the actual time spent on certain types of work differs from the intended split you can react quickly and take steps to adjust the balance of your time.

Use a computer?

The planning and managing of a multiple project environment can be made easier by using a computer system (see Chapter 13). However, the computer system will probably only point out clashes between projects; it will not help very much with the initial planning.

Summary

SP is a method for managing a small project. However, its underlying principles are completely valid in the multiple project environment within which most of us work.

CHAPTER TWELVE

Managing a Crisis

There will be crises, despite your careful following of all the guidelines encapsulated within SP. No project management method can overcome all the unknowns; no author can write a series of guidelines in such a way that any reader can be guaranteed perfect success every time. So, I've got the cop-out in at last!

Make it worse; make it better

We all know that in a crisis there are things we can do that make it worse. Well, there are things we can do to make it better too, things that help us get the crisis back under control.

I suppose that this chapter is a condensed version of the whole book. In a crisis there are a few basic but vital factors that you must manage. The difficulty is recognising them in amongst the smoke and the yelling that accompanies most crises.

Vital few from trivial many

The theme of SP is sorting the Vital Few things to do from the Trivial Many. Here is how to do this for a crisis situation.

Do you really have crises?

First of all, just what is a crisis? If you attempt a definition by listing the attributes of a crisis, a strategy for their management should emerge. Such attributes are usually stated as:

- something unplanned or unforeseen

- very tight timescales, usually forced on us

- changes to resources

- changes to objectives or scope (what we were aiming at, or the size of the job)

Those macho types among us will claim, or even boast, that they live in crisis mode all the time. Well, I wonder about that. If it is true then maybe our personal prioritisation rules need to be examined. Just being busy – even rushed off our feet – does not signify crisis.

I am talking about organisation-threatening events that spring upon you (substitute life, job or whatever is important to you). The concept of dealing with factors forced upon us within a tight timescale is a common working definition of a crisis.

So what are the vital few elements that must be managed at all costs:

- objectives and constraints

- plans

- roles and responsibilities

- communication

- and, unusually for this book, a few words about behaviour!

Behaviour

Let us start with behaviour. How you act can have a major impact in a crisis, as there is so little time to recover from mistakes. Some don'ts:

- Don't panic, or rather, don't panic visibly. Panic is contagious; if people see you panicking then they will panic as well. You can be in turmoil inside, but don't let it show. Calm control is just as contagious; I know which one I'd rather catch. Don't attempt to dispel thoughts of panic by lounging about, though; it is a matter of balance.

- Don't rush into a course of action you will regret later. (This often creates several more crises out of the original one.) We will look later at what to do to find out facts, but jumping to conclusions without any research is very dangerous.

- Don't be afraid to ask for help; although some people revel in hearing about your problems, most people are willing to help. There might just be somebody who has been through this exact crisis before. Bottling things up can be very dangerous.

The crisis checklist

And now, a basic checklist. Analyse the situation as coolly as possible. Establish the following:

- What is actually happening, as opposed to what is being shouted about?

- Why it is happening (develop a theory; get facts; test theory; try again)?

- How quickly do you have to act before things get seriously worse (especially look for timescales on stopping it spreading or containment activities)?

- What might happen if you do nothing?

- Who else is involved?

- Who else might get dragged in?

- What resources do you have available?

This list may seem long, even too much to waste time on. The clever answer to that is 'How much time do you think you have to waste?' Without going through this checklist, you will be fighting in the dark.

In reality, you may find that the checklist takes all too short a time; you might wish you had more questions to ask.

Now, having asked the questions, tackle the information in this way – draw up a preliminary action plan, based around three levels of priority:

1. **Interim measures:** What has to be done to stop it from getting worse?

2. **Adaptive measures:** What could be done to help us carry on 'normal' business in the new circumstances?

3. **Corrective measures:** What has to be done to fix the underlying problem that caused the crisis?

Keep your mind clearly focused on the relative priorities. Don't start a philosophical discussion on pollution-free, non-combustible building materials (corrective measures) while the building is still on fire – try some interim measures (i.e. put the fire out).

Rules for a simple plan

Some people enjoy a philosophical discussion at any time, even in a burning building, especially if it is your problem to sort out rather than theirs. You must establish a public mechanism for directing and controlling everyone's efforts. This will be a plan of some sort, but there are three golden rules for a crisis plan:

1. **Keep it simple**; otherwise, nobody will understand it, and you won't keep it up to date.

2. **Keep it public** so that you can remind the drifters to get back to the point in question.

3. **Update it with new info** because it must change as you move through the crisis.

Real roles work

Review roles and responsibilities, especially from the viewpoint 'Do we really need all these people involved?' If someone has a clear and genuine role they will fulfil it splendidly; if they don't, they will be in the way.

Check your own levels of authority. Do you really have the authority to turn off the main power to the office block?

When the 'phone starts to ring'

Open simple lines of communication. As soon as people find out that you are dealing with the crisis, your phone will not stop ringing with their inquiries, help, offers of assistance, requests for progress reports, a suggestion that you speak to the press, and so on. It is inevitable, but if you are trying to play a real part in solving the crisis, you will find the interruptions highly damaging.

So, set up a communications centre – someone to answer the phones. Let everyone know that this has been done.

Make sure that the project or crisis team keep the communications centre up to date with the situation. In this way the communications person will be able to field a large proportion of incoming calls, freeing you and the team to get on with the work.

Make plans for handling your own normal work and that of the crisis team members. You don't want to create a new crisis out of this one.

Stand back at least once a day and review how things are going against the 'plan.'

Monitor your actions

As soon as you take action, monitor its effects. Set up a monitoring mechanism that will last until the crisis is over. None of this will guarantee that you will manage your way through all the crises that come your way, but if you do tackle them in an orderly manner, people will see that you are trying.

CHAPTER THIRTEEN

Using a Computer
(Don't do it!)

Seriously, why would you want to use a computer to help you manage a small project? As this is a serious question, let me offer some serious answers:

- Firstly, you have a project which is unclear at the start and you want to list a few tasks to get you going, knowing full well that as soon as you start lots of other tasks will come creeping out of the woodwork. You reason that, if the plan is stored on a computer, you can easily add the new tasks when they appear.

- Secondly, you have a project which requires a publishable plan, either to the Sponsor or maybe to an outside Customer, and you feel that a plan printed by a computer might look better than a handwritten list.

- Thirdly, you have heard a lot about the new project management software that's on the market and you want to get something to help you as much as possible; after all, there must be something to it.

- Fourthly, you fancy playing with a computer package that will produce lovely looking plans, etc.

- Lastly, the boss says 'use this piece of software to manage your project,' so you have to at least give it a try.

Am I getting close?

No advertisements!

This chapter is aimed at dispelling the myths about project planning systems, setting some guidelines for what to look for if you have to choose one and describing how to use one: a generic one, not a specific one – I'm not advertising anybody's software for them.

I am a fan

If this chapter begins to sound like a diatribe against planning packages then let me declare right away that I'm not against them. I think that they can be of great assistance to a project manager. What really does worry me, though, is the way that many bosses think that, once they have allowed you to purchase some planning software, you can produce effective project plans.

Tools do not equal skills

If you were to give me a set of chisels it wouldn't make me into a carpenter; just a person with a set of chisels. If the chisels are sharp then I become a dangerous person. Training in how to use chisels does not make me into a carpenter; just into a skilled chiseller.

Giving a novice project manager a piece of project planning software does not make that project manager into a skilled planner, just a person with a piece of software. Training in the software merely makes the person proficient in the software, not a skilled project planner.

GIGO

Unfortunately, the software will produce some seductively well-presented documents that look like project plans, but do you remember the old saying 'GIGO' meaning 'Garbage In, Garbage Out?' Well, when applied to plans it means 'Garbage In, Gospel Out.' If you don't know what a project plan should contain and how it should be constructed, the use of a piece of software will be dangerous; you will produce something that looks so good people will believe it.

It can help a little

When making decisions about planning the steps in a project (Chapter 4) a computer cannot help much, especially with:

- compiling a list of tasks
- getting them into a sensible sequence

163

- breaking them into practical units

- estimating size and cost

- identifying resources required

- assigning resources to tasks

- allowing for contingency

Planning tools, or management tools

While we are on the subject of putting a planning tool into context, many of them are sold as Project Management Packages. Don't be misled by this, people manage projects not computers. Here is a list of the topics that a project manager should consider when managing a project. Again, a computer is not a lot of help with management decisions:

- Initiation

- Strategic project factors

- Shaping the project into phases

- Project definition

- Roles & responsibilities

- Estimating

- Budgeting

- Managing risk

- Controlling the project

- Measuring progress

- Interpreting progress information

- Replanning the project

- Planning for quality

- Measuring quality

- Managing change

- Reviewing the project

- Managing several projects at once

- Managing a crisis

Where it can help

Now, let us focus on what a piece of planning software can do. In manipulating the plan it can:

- hold the list of tasks so that you can update it

- hold a list of resources so that you can update it

- hold target dates, and remind you when events linked to dates are due

- draw and redraw bar charts or Gantt Charts easily

- make many copies of complex lists and charts

- extract tasks applicable to particular individuals to provide each team member with their own plan

- provide version control of plans so that confusion over versions can be minimised

- warn you of a resource overload so that a key person is not accidentally over-assigned

- allow you to produce timesheets or worksheets for individuals

- capture actual time spent (and therefore the actual cost incurred)

- allow you to merge several separate plans together and identify resource usage across them so that potential resource problems can be spotted before they occur

- recalculate costs and timescales for work not completed

- print project plans at a summary level to help senior management to operate without being swamped by the tiny details

- record the thought processes and working details against each task so that we don't forget why something was done in a particular way

- … and so on.

Actually, the list is quite impressive so far. There are many more things that can be done, varying from package to package.

But you must know what you are doing

So, I hope that I sound a bit more positive now. I really do think that they can be very useful, but only after the user, be it the project manager, specialist project planner, or whoever, has been shown capable of producing effective project plans 'by hand.' By this, I mean that the users of such software must know exactly what they require and how they can do it before they attempt to get a computer system to help them.

One last analogy and then I will become positive and stay positive. You wouldn't buy an accounting package, give it to a novice and then rely on them to produce company accounts for the next month end, would you?

If you turn back to my earlier list of planning steps, you can begin to see how you can use a computer to really help:

- **Compile a list of tasks** - Not the creative bit, but software can help in several ways:

  - template plans

  - recording what you did last time so that if your current project is similar, you may be able to give yourself a head start by amending a previous plan

  - reminding you of the standard tasks you must include (or at least, consider for inclusion) if your project must follow a standard pattern

- **Get them into a sensible sequence** - To extend the theme from above, your 'starter' plan (sometimes called a template plan) could also include likely sequences.

- **Break them into practical units** - Ditto.

- **Estimate their size/cost** - Ditto for estimates.

- **Identify resources required** - Ditto for resources.

- **Assign resources to tasks** - It may be possible to build a library of resources (people, machines, etc.) that you can call up in every project plan. You don't have to use them all the time but once you have the library, you can incorporate it into whichever plans you desire. It may also be advantageous to record against each resource their capability (but watch out for privacy legislation implications). Individual cost rates can also be entered to help with automatic project cost calculations. The ability to record and reuse individual availabilities is also very helpful.

- **Allow for contingency** - There's not a lot that a planning tool can do here except to help store details of what actually happened last time.

Now, take a look at some of the types of software that might be of use. You must take a realistic view of the type and level of planning you will actually carry out.

Word processor

Don't spend time and money installing a powerful planning package if you will probably only want to create and maintain a list of tasks, together with their associated target dates and resources. A word processing system will almost certainly be sufficient for this type of planning; simple to learn, simple to use, fit for the purpose.

If you want to progress to any of the following:

- bar charts
- weekly resource usage and costs

- merging of several detailed plans into one consolidated plan

- critical path analysis and Gantt Charts

then you should consider these factors before you fire up your sophisticated planning software:

- **Something fancier** – Does the size of the project really justify this level of planning?

  - less than 4 weeks – almost certainly not

  - 4-8 weeks – possibly not

  - more than 8 weeks – probably

- **Practical considerations** – Do you have the computer system to do it effectively? Consider performance, accessibility, and portability (if you will be doing most of your work on several different sites, where do you want the plan to be?)

- **Learning on a live project** – Do you really have the skills? Will you spend a disproportionate amount of time learning and struggling, only to make a subtle yet dangerous mistake?

If, after considering all the pros and cons, you decide to go ahead, here are a few simple tips to ease the process:

- **Conventions** - Establish and stick to a common naming convention for your resources; to a software package JS, J S, Jim and Jim Smith are four different resources, and each will be allocated to the maximum; poor old Jim Smith!

- **Hours per week** - Be realistic with people's likely availability for project work (most people would find it difficult to give you more than three days per week, or four to five hours per day).

- **Holidays** - Make sure you build in fixed events first; public holidays, personal holidays, and company events.

- **Blocks** - Group your tasks into meaningful blocks; this could be very useful when you come to print out the plan, as you could choose to print only at the 'summary' level, in order to see an uncluttered view of the project.

- **Printer** - Use the printer often; it can be very easy to lose sight of the project if your view is limited to a small window somewhere in the middle of a screen.

- **Notes** - Use the built-in note facility if there is one; record as many of your thought processes as you can; do whatever you can while you are building the plan so that in three weeks you don't find yourself saying 'Now why did I do that?'

I'm sure that there are many more hints and tips; read the manual that comes with the software for tips that are specific to the package you intend to use.

Now go for it

Let me repeat something I said earlier; I am a fan of PC-based planning tools, but only because I know how to produce a project plan. Don't think that the tool, however sophisticated, will let you off the problems of project management. Don't expect too much, but they can be of valuable assistance.

CHAPTER FOURTEEN

Implementing the SP Method

So, you've read the book. Do you really want to implement SP? You must ask yourself 'Why?' Which aspects of your current operation are you hoping to improve?

It is very important that you are clear about this. Without such targets, you could just fritter away your efforts in a haphazard fashion. In fact, you should view the implementation of SP as a project in its own right and a project needs:

- objectives

- a plan

- roles and responsibilities

- resources

Treat it as a project

At the end of this chapter, you will find a typical project definition for implementing SP. Remember, it is only a typical example and would need tuning to meet your own circumstances. We will now look at how to tune the example plan.

SP begins with Strategic Project Factors. Here are a few questions for you to consider:

- **Who will be responsible?** Who will be involved in this implementation project? Who will manage it? Who else might be involved in drawing up specific guidelines or standards?

- **Who will be involved?** Who will use SP? How much training will they need (training in SP or training in project management as well)?

- **By when?** What is the time scale for implementing SP? In phases, or in a big bang approach?

- **Any risks?** Anyone using something like SP for the first time will probably take a little longer that they used to take; this must be allowed for and any potential sufferers of this delay should be warned.

- **Scope of SP?** Who will use SP? When? On what type of projects? Will every project over two days long adopt SP?

Organise the SP project

Consider the organisation behind the project:

- **Nominate a Sponsor**: make sure the Sponsor knows the objectives, the proposed process of implementation, and his or her role in it.

- **Choose a Project Manager**: consider his or her credibility. (Sometimes a project manager from outside the organisation has better credibility.)

- **Identify other interested parties**: for example, personnel and training, internal and external customers, sales, marketing, etc.

An outline plan

Here is an outline plan for the implementation of SP:

- Appoint a Sponsor and Project Manager.

- Identify target SP players.

- Identify individual implementation opportunities. Don't put a person working on a very high risk project straight onto SP for their first project.

- Identify individual training needs.

- Initiate project management training.

- Order SP copies.

- Initiate training.

- Implement.

- Monitor performance.

- Consider the follow-up: SP clinics, a help desk, or a centre of competence.

Extra plan for PC tools

If you are going to use a PC to help with the planning process:

- Replace/upgrade your hardware.

- Install the software.

- Implement software training.

- Implement the first few projects.

- Review the results.

- Roll out the service to other project managers.

Monitoring progress

This must be tied very closely to your objectives. There are some simple numerical checks you could carry out:

- Does every project over two days long have a Project Definition?

- Is every Project Definition up to date (or, being realistic, no more than three days out of date)?

- Does every project over two days long have a Sponsor and a Project Manager?

Follow it up

The next step (and this should be handled with a little tact, so as not to appear to be too interrogatory):

- Select a Project Manager who has implemented SP.

- Ask to see the Project Definitions.

- Validate: ask to be shown the project and see how well the definition reflects what is happening on the project.

Review the scope

This only leaves 'other work,' and some of this maybe should be managed with SP. Unless your people fill in timesheets (from which large slabs of non-SP project time can be identified), or you have an encyclopaedic knowledge of their activities, you can only pick up whether they are using SP on every appropriate opportunity by observation.

Potential problems

Here are some common problems with implementing SP, together with some suggested fixes:

- **Projects are 'too large' for SP.** So what are you using instead? SP will be better than nothing, even on a large project. There are methodologies around for large projects if you really want to formalise such jobs. Alternatively, see Appendix C for information on 'larger' methods.

- **Projects are 'too small' for SP.** Don't use SP. Make sure that these 'small projects' actually are projects in their own right. Maybe they are tasks from some other, bigger, piece of work, which should be in the system.

- **SP is taking too much time.** Yes, it will take longer at first. If it is still taking too long after, say, 10 projects, consider the following:

  - **Scrap it** – it doesn't fit your environment (but what is so special about your environment?)

  - **Change personnel** – is your Project Manager up to it, motivated, committed?

  - **Review the training** – maybe more coaching or formal training will do it

  - **Tune SP** – maybe your environment is such that certain parts of SP really are too time-consuming.

- **Projects still fail.** Start collecting honest facts; are your Project Managers being given enough time and support to do a good job?

- **It works in our pilot projects and we want to roll it out, but we have too many people to train.** Training in SP is not difficult and there are no copyright problems. So your training people could develop and run the training, thereby cutting costs.

- **We started using SP, but it has now faded out.** You must find out why this has happened. This type of fade out is not unique to SP (remember the fuss and hype over ISO 9000?) If there are structural or procedural problems with SP then call for assistance with tuning and re-implementation. Otherwise, review your management commitment. If your management is not committed to a methodology such as SP, how can you expect your project management staff to maintain their commitment?

- **Demonstrating management commitment.** How can you demonstrate management commitment? Here are some suggestions to help you re-establish the visible management commitment to SP:

    - Insist upon Project Definitions and sign them off.

    - Carry out spot checks of Project Definitions.

    - Respect their Project Definitions, even if you have doubts; let them run their projects according to their own Project Definitions.

    - Review Project Definitions during your regular progress meetings.

    - Use Project Definitions yourself.

    - Make Project Definitions public; get each Project Manager to post the Project Definitions on a notice board for all to see.

- **We've just merged with XYZ and they use their own project management approach. Should we switch to theirs, or force SP on them?** Firstly, SP is unusual in that it is specifically designed for smaller projects. Are the XYZ people actually using their approach on smaller projects? Maybe you should be looking at a two-tier approach, with SP for all smaller projects and the XYZ method for all larger jobs. If you can prove the business benefits of SP then you might be able to convince them to switch to SP.

Proving the business benefits

The business benefits of implementing SP are:

- Control over the mass of smaller projects that make up the greater part of business life

- Facts about progress, risks and achievements

- Assurance that the right end product is being produced, to cost and time targets

- Early warning of potential problems, with options for dealing with them

Measuring the achievement of these benefits should not be left to a 'How do we feel about this?' type of subjective measurement. If you are serious about improving your project management effectiveness, you should try to set up some objective measures.

Measuring the benefits

Simple measures

- How many people should be using SP?

- How many people are using SP?

- How many projects are being managed using SP (i.e. How many have Project Definition Forms)?

- How many projects also have one or more of the optional forms (Risk Assessment, Change Management Sheet, Project Quality Plan, Project Budget)?

- How many smaller projects are there that are not controlled by SP (and why not)?

Effectiveness

- Ask senior management

- Do you feel in better control over the mass of smaller projects you have delegated to Project Managers?

- Why, or why not

- Are you receiving regular factual progress reports?

- Are the company's projects finishing on time, on budget, meeting business requirements, more often than they used to?

- Are you being warned of potential problems before they occur?

Managing Smaller Projects: A Practical Guide

Ask project managers

- Do you feel in control of your portfolio of projects?

- Why or why not?

- Are the overheads of SP worthwhile?

- Why or why not?

What next?

Congratulations on reaching this far! I am glad that I have been able to keep your interest for all these pages. I hope that you are now mulling over what you should do to implement SP. The forms in Appendix A are provided copyright free for to you to use as you see fit. They contain the elements that you need to control your smaller projects effectively.

I believe that there are considerable business benefits to be gained from applying good project management practice. You may well find that as your projects cross that grey borderline between small and large, you will need to adopt more sophisticated tools and techniques. However, the basic principles set out here will still hold good as you widen your horizon to explore the world of project management still further.

182

CHAPTER FIFTEEN

Managing Stakeholders

There have been many surveys into reasons why projects don't always go as planned (The Standish Group in the US and KPMG in the UK conduct such surveys regularly), and their findings are quite depressing. Actually, what is even more depressing is that these findings haven't changed in the 35-year period that the surveys have been running.

Anyway, the findings can be paraphrased as follows: most projects perform badly, not because of some hugely difficult technical problems, but because the expectations and commitment of key players had been badly handled. People expected one thing, the project delivered something else, and no-one was ready for the outcome.

I'm sure we can all think of large well-known projects that we could classify as 'failures,' but with a bit of thought we might also admit that we 'could have told them it was doomed from the start.'

So why do we classify them as failures? I contend that part of the reason is to do with how our expectations have been badly handled. Hence stakeholder management!

What is a stakeholder?

There is a classic definition of 'stakeholder' supplied by the Association of Project Management. It says that a stakeholder is anyone upon whom the project can have an effect, and anyone who can affect the project.

I suppose that covers just about anybody involved in a project and, in fact, the width of the definition is a deliberate attempt to force Project Managers to think widely about just who has to be considered and 'managed' in a project.

Some examples

So, a list of stakeholders in a project ought to include:

- Our Project Customer, on whom the project must certainly have an effect

- The Project Sponsor, who can have a large effect on the project

- The end users of whatever our project is trying to deliver; it must surely affect them

- Suppliers, of labour or materials, who by their actions (or inaction) can affect the project

- Any regulatory or official bodies on whom we rely for approvals

- Our project team members, if there are any (we may be the Project Manager and the only resource, so we are the stakeholder in this case)

- Our colleagues, who may be supplying us with resources, assistance, or advice

Why do we need to manage them?

Most Project Managers think about their stakeholders only after some huge problem has occurred, and they need to know to whom they should apologise. It is usually not productive to be approaching stakeholders for the first time in this recovery situation.

Stakeholder management tries to sort out problems like this before they occur, by identifying who the stakeholders are, identifying their likely attitudes towards our project, and taking actions in the project which might get them on-side and keep them on-side throughout the whole project.

If we can build an environment around the project that stakeholders perceive as something that might be good for them, then we may be enrolling them as allies.

If we make no positive attempt to manage our stakeholders' attitudes and perceptions then we are at the mercy of fate as our project unfolds.

Is it free?

On the types of small project within the scope of the SP
method, then stakeholder management may not cost much,
but it may not be completely free. As described below, a key
component of stakeholder management is that of action
planning. This will give rise to new tasks designed to turn our
stakeholders into positive enthusiasts. These tasks may have
resource and cost implications, so the cost of the project may
rise.

This in turn may mean that the Project Manager will
have to explain to the Sponsor why more resources (financial or
human) are required. A carefully prepared stakeholder
management plan (see opposite) will be invaluable in this
regard.

Don't forget, on very large projects (for example the
Channel Tunnel and its associated rail links) the project
management team may well engage professionals to undertake
stakeholder management for them. Public relations specialists
may set about trying to manage the expectations of key groups
of stakeholders (for example, the residents affected by
construction). This sort of stakeholder management is
definitely not free!

What does a stakeholder management plan look like?

Form SP7 is a typical stakeholder management plan. It is just a
simple form, drawn up by the Project Manager, documenting
his or her analysis of who the stakeholders are and what he or
she plans to do to manage them.

<table>
<tr><td colspan="5">SP7 STAKEHOLDER MANAGEMENT PLAN</td></tr>
<tr><td>Stakeholder name</td><td>Impact</td><td>Attitude</td><td colspan="2">Actions</td></tr>
</table>

Stakeholder name	Impact	Attitude	Actions

It would normally be completed during the initiation stage of the project, and the form would be filed together with the Project Definition documents.

Do all projects need this? Well, no, but… All projects have stakeholders, and many projects, however small, can end up upsetting or disappointing them. So, even in a small project it might be worth setting aside a few minutes during the initiation stage to think about the stakeholders and to try to identify ways in which you can run the project to deliver stakeholder satisfaction.

How do we manage stakeholders?

The process of stakeholder management has four components, all of which take place initially at the start of the project. They are as described below.

Stakeholder identification

This is an ideal opportunity to involve other project team members, if there are any. Raise their awareness and interest in the project by getting them to brainstorm a list of stakeholders. If you have no project team then just sit and think of the list yourself.

You are trying to identify all those people affected by, or affecting, the project. Look at the Project Definition, and whatever other documents you have, and visualise the project running from start to end. Note down all the people touched by the project, whether or not you think they are important (we'll judge this later). Keep to the classic brainstorming rules, that is, NO filtering at this stage.

There are some stakeholders that are traditionally completely overlooked. For example, your boss is a key stakeholder in your project, even if he/she is not involved as the Sponsor. Think how much of an effect the boss can have just by changing your priorities around a little.

Evaluation of impact

Some stakeholders hold more stake than others. Some can really hinder the project, while others might have only a marginal effect. So, once the list is complete, go back and assess each stakeholder for potential impact using a simple high/medium/low assessment method.

When you get to the action planning stage you will be able to focus your efforts on the high-impact stakeholders first.

Evaluation of attitude

This part of the process is more tricky. You need to identify the likely attitude of each stakeholder towards your project. You are trying to identify allies and opponents, as the actions you intend to take in the action planning step depend upon where you think each stakeholder might be coming from. Don't assume that just because you are really excited about the project all the other key players will be in a similar positive frame of mind.

It may be necessary to go so far as to ask key stakeholders exactly what they are looking for out of the project. Try to communicate to them the constructive view that you will try to deliver not only the end result but also satisfied stakeholders. If this works, then they may be more open in expressing their concerns or desires for the project.

In any case, if you never ask, you'll never find out... until it's too late.

Action planning

Having gone to the trouble of identifying stakeholders and assessing their potential impact, and so on, it would be daft not to do something about them. So, action planning is the part of stakeholder management in which the Project Manager can become creative and constructive. You must identify actions you could take during the project that are specifically aimed at key stakeholders (initially, the high-impact ones), and that will take them from awareness, through interest, into commitment. Once you've identified some actions, you must add them into the main project plan, otherwise you may forget to carry them out (and wouldn't that be annoying for all concerned).

Just what actions might be appropriate? Usually, you can't positively motivate someone just by not upsetting them, so action planning must include a little more than 'deliver the end result as requested,' 'minimise disruption,' or whatever.

These things are important, but we must think of some more positive actions to take that will have the stakeholders really engaged in the project.

Many really effective actions are little more than just good communications, but others might include:

- Inviting a stakeholder to a working demo

- Inviting the stakeholder to take some responsibility for the publicity surrounding the project

- Getting a stakeholder to deliver some of the training, if appropriate

- Keeping stakeholders informed at every step of the way

- Giving them early warning of problems, and involving them in any solution

- Discussing your risk management strategy with them

Monitoring our success

Just because you drew up a stakeholder management plan and kicked off some actions doesn't mean that any of them will work as you hope. You've got to monitor the effect of your actions, and make adjustments where necessary.

Observe the effect your actions are having on the various stakeholders, and keep up the good work.

CHAPTER SIXTEEN

Managing e-Commerce Projects

The SP Method encompasses smaller projects in almost any area of business and commerce including those involved with newer, high-tech projects.

What are e-commerce projects?

There is nothing inherently new about e-commerce projects, but the environment surrounding them has several characteristics that will influence the way they should be managed. The SP method is uniquely suited to managing such projects, for reasons which will emerge later.

Typical types of e-commerce projects include:

- Building on a package, such as creating one-to-one marketing for a website

- Web design and website creation

- Website performance monitoring and improvements

- Developing a web-based application; for example, an e-commerce site linked directly to a database for maintaining a sales catalogue, capturing customer orders, processing payments, and so on.

What characteristics do they have?

The features that distinguish an e-commerce project from other more traditional types of project include:

- The speed of delivery – Usually speed is paramount because of perceived or actual business pressures.

- Scarce technical resources, and unfamiliar ways of employing such resources (contractors, freelancers, or outsourcing to another specialist company)

- Internal customers may have little or no idea of the possibilities for the scope of the final design, and may have no clear understanding of their role in the project.

- Unclear business objectives from the outset, leading to a large number of changes as the requirements emerge

- Some commercial components may be in the very early stages of their life cycle (it is not unusual to attempt to build a service that is vital to one's own business based on brand-new, poorly-tested software).

192

- No history of similar projects, so no guidelines, however informal

- Highly technical Project Manager and project team

- So-called Rapid Application Development methods attempted, but by inexperienced or poorly-managed staff

- Changing technology, so the temptation to allow 'scope creep.'

What are the implications for management?

There are several important implications that must be understood and accepted by the business once e-commerce developments are undertaken.

- **Non-error-free delivery**. One of the main principals of iterative developments is that while the target date is unmovable, the scope of what is considered an acceptable end product will change (i.e. reduce) during the project. All those concerned must realise that a tight delivery date can be met only by accepting a reduced end product and, quite possibly, an end product with errors in it. Once this principle is accepted, the project can plan for how to deal with what gets dropped off, or what will need tweaking after delivery.

- **Stakeholders**. As one might expect, the stakeholders will have to play a full part in this type of project, especially if the way in which scope is reduced is badly handled. Very close and constructive links with stakeholders will be major factors in the success of the project.

- **Support**. If, as stated earlier, the end product could be delivered in an incomplete state, arrangements for post-delivery support must be created and developed as an integral part of the project, not tacked on as an afterthought.

- **Adjust and modify goals**. There must be a simple and swift mechanism for dealing with proposed changes in goals, scope, budget, and so on. The process must encourage full participation by all relevant decision-makers without slowing the project down. There must be a documented audit trail of decisions, and nothing must be simply dropped out of sight.

Why do we need to manage them in a particular manner?

In circumstances like these it is very tempting for a project manager to 'just do it.' Unfortunately, some project managers get mixed up, and think that heroes are created from superhuman effort, and they forget that achievement plays a major part in defining a hero.

A classic mistake made by technical project managers at this stage is to decide that, in order to speed things up (the project clock is ticking, remember), the best thing to do is to keep the customer out of the way, and deliver a fully working, comprehensive outcome.

It always seems to techies that it is the customer who slows things down, by changing their requirements in midstream. So, if the customer is excluded, then this will remove a major source of delay.

Obviously, this can be true during the project, but as soon as the end product is delivered then the dam bursts, and the project team is overwhelmed with requests for changes.

How do people manage traditional projects?

Most successful projects begin with getting the outline plan sorted out (often called the 'structure', or 'the approach'), and many people rely on a methodology to help them identify the structure. A methodology consists of a set of processes, tasks, role descriptions and guidelines covering all that might happen in a project.

Most methodologies are used to reduce the risk involved in making up a project approach fresh every time, by building on the experience of others. There are many methodologies around, covering such diverse activities as shipbuilding, motorway construction, and computer systems development.

Unfortunately, most methodologies aimed at computer systems development have been around for a long time. This means that they are tried and tested, but are not immediately useful for modern e-commerce methods.

What characterises traditional approaches to systems development is the step-by-step way of detailing user requirements, drawing up a business design, then preparing a computer system design. This is then followed by coding and testing the system, acceptance testing, and implementation.

Such an approach might look like this:

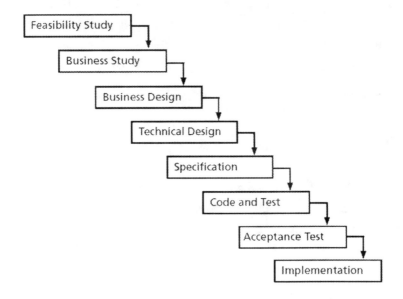

Not surprisingly, this style of approach is called the 'waterfall' method, as information flows downhill, from one completed stage to the next.

This is a very safe way of building a computer system, as each stage relies on the previous stage being signed off. However, it can be a very slow and painstaking way of creating computer systems, as the pieces of work can only happen one after the other.

Many e-commerce system development projects use a prototyping or iterative development approach, meaning that the developers jump straight to coding and testing the system, with the users sitting alongside approving or rejecting components of the design as they emerge.

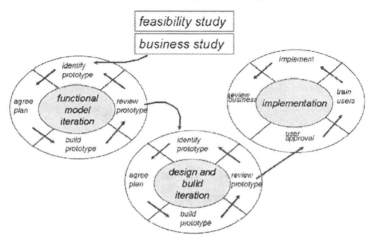

iterative development approach

This style of development needs a different style of management, but many of the basic elements of such a project are the same as the traditional approach. For example, both approaches begin with a feasibility study and a business study.

The main differences, however, centre on the roles and responsibilities and the prototyping loops. The amount of time spent in these loops must be carefully managed, but the key to a successful prototyping project lies in the clear understanding of the roles and responsibilities of all concerned. For example, the key customer roles must be filled by people assigned to the project full-time, and they must have authority to accept or reject prototypes without recourse to other management levels.

The detail of such a methodology is beyond the scope and objectives of this book, but for more information refer to the website of the DSDM Consortium: www.dsdm.com. DSDM stands for Dynamic Systems Development Methodology, and is a successful and highly professional approach to iterative developments. It contains guidelines on how to manage the technical aspects of such projects, as well as detailed descriptions of the technical processes. However, many development teams don't use formal methods such as DSDM, so the provisions of the SP method can be of great benefit to them.

What sort of project management is required/appropriate?

In general, e-commerce projects need a low-bureaucracy high-security methodology, in that the technical project team needs low bureaucracy (so as not to slow the project down) while the customers and management need high security (so as to increase the chances of a successful outcome).

The flexibility of the SP method fits the bill perfectly, as follows:

- **Project definition**. Using the Project Definition form the team can quickly establish the first cut of the main project parameters (objectives, scope, and constraints) and use this agreed definition as the baseline against which to manage all changes.

- **Risk management.** All projects will benefit from a simple, structured approach to risk identification, assessment and management.

- **Quality management.** Defining and agreeing just what is meant by quality in the context of a specific project can be difficult; the clear SP process speeds up this part of defining the project.

- **Project planning.** With a prototyping approach to application development, a clear project plan is vital; the simplicity of SP aids the drawing up of an effective plan.

- **Change management.** As soon as the project starts (or, probably, even earlier than that during the definition process) the project team will be under pressure to make changes; the SP Change Management form will enable the team to stay in control of the changes, rather than being swamped by them.

- **Stakeholder management.** One of the key components to a successful e-commerce project is positive and constructive stakeholder management; the SP process will produce a good basis for this management.

Summary

E-commerce projects can be an excuse for hacking, in that techies can carve out lumps of a computer system without any discipline, all in the name of speed of delivery. Unfortunately, projects managed in such a manner merely rush the whole project team straight to the scene of the accident, and either the whole thing has to be scrapped, or a monster is delivered, which costs an arm and a leg to sort out after implementation.

A more thoughtful project approach will save time and money almost from day one, and enable an organisation to take business advantage of new technology.

SP Forms

SP1 Project Definition

SP2 Project Risk Assessment

SP3 Change Management

SP4 Budget Plan for Project

SP5 Project Quality Plan

SP6 Project Phase/Task List

SP7 Stakeholder Management Plan

SP1 PROJECT DEFINITION

Project Name and Brief Description

Project Outline

Objectives • What is the project designed to achieve

Scope • What is included, what is excluded

Constraints

Roles and Responsibilities • Project Sponsor, Customer, Manager

Main Products/Deliverables • What is to be produced, in what form

External Dependencies • Links to other projects

Underlying Assumptions

Project Phases/Tasks

Phase/Task	Resource	Start Date	End Date	Status

Project Review Points

Date or Project Event	Review Deliverable	Review Method	Actual Status

Approvals/Authorisation

	name:	approval to begin: date:	completion: date:
Project Sponsor			
Project Manager			
Project Customer			

	reqd?		reqd?
Risk Assessment		Project Quality Plan	
Change Management Sheet		Project Budget	

SP2 PROJECT RISK ASSESSMENT

Project Name and Brief Description

Compiled By: Date:

Approved By: Date:

Risk:

Preventive Actions:

Contingent Actions:

Trigger Actions:

Risk:

Preventive Actions:

Contingent Actions:

Trigger Actions:

Risk:

Preventive Actions:

Contingent Actions:

Trigger Actions:

Risk:

Preventive Actions:

Contingent Actions:

Trigger Actions:

Risk:

Preventive Actions:

Contingent Actions:

Trigger Actions:

SP3 CHANGE MANAGEMENT

Project Name and Brief Description

Compiled By: Date:

Change:

Implications:

Accepted By: date:

Change:

Implications:

Accepted By: date:

Change:

Implications:

Accepted By: date:

Change:

Implications:

Accepted By: date:

Change:

Implications:

Accepted By: date:

Change:

Implications:

Accepted By: date:

Change:

Implications:

Accepted By: date:

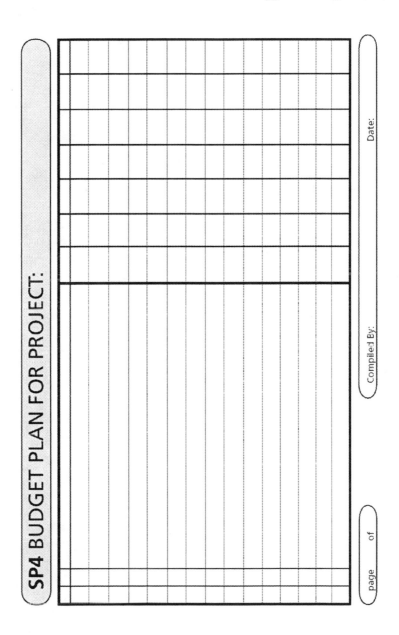

SP4 BUDGET PLAN FOR PROJECT:

page   of

Compiled By:

Date:

SP5 PROJECT QUALITY PLAN

Project Name and Brief Description

Compiled By: Date:

Approved By: Date:

Quality Targets:

Prioritised targets against which the success of the project will be judged, e.g. Delivery Date, Development Cost, Quality of Product. The latter must be expressed in specific terms, based upon Functionality, Usability, Reliability, Performance, Serviceability

Accepted By: Date:

Approach to be used:

Standards, Methods, Technologies, Tools. Justification of deviation from normal standards

Implementation Strategy:

Outline of method of implementation, including implications of strategies such as parallel or pilot implementations

Major Products to be Reviewed

Product: target review date:

Review Method:

Findings: actual review date:

Corrective Action Required:

Action Taken By: corrective action date:

Product: target review date:

Review Method:

Findings: actual review date:

Corrective Action Required:

Action Taken By: corrective action date:

SP6 PROJECT PHASE/TASK LIST

Project Name and Brief Description

Project Phases/Tasks

Phase/Task	Resource	Start Date	End Date	Status

SP7 STAKEHOLDER MANAGEMENT PLAN

Stakeholder name	Impact	Attitude	Actions

SP Checklists

Checklist 1: Starting the Project

Checklist 2: Running the Project

Checklist 1 • Starting the Project

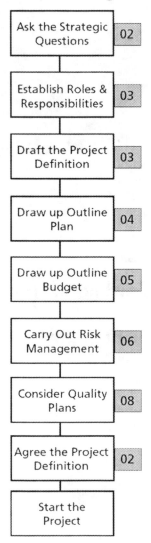

Ask the Strategic Questions	02
Establish Roles & Responsibilities	03
Draft the Project Definition	03
Draw up Outline Plan	04
Draw up Outline Budget	05
Carry Out Risk Management	06
Consider Quality Plans	08
Agree the Project Definition	02
Start the Project	

Checklist 2 • Running the Project

Indicates the relevant Chapter number

Methods

F or larger projects, there is a larger choice of methodologies. The two main global contenders in the medium-to-large project arena are PRINCE2™ and those based upon the PMBoK.™

PRINCE2 is a process-based project management methodology developed on behalf of the UK Government. It is freely available in the public domain, and offers a comprehensive set of project management processes. It is accompanied by the full panoply of methodology support, including training, examinations and qualifications. For more information see http://www.ogc.gov.uk.

PMBoK stands for the Project Management Body of Knowledge, which is published by the Project Management Institute (PMI), a US-based organization recognised as the key global player in professional project management.

The PMBoK itself is not really a methodology; it is more an in-depth explanation of everything a project manager needs to know to run a project. It too is accompanied by training, examinations and qualifications. However, many organizations have built their project management processes around the structure provided by the PMBoK.

Both of these approaches to project management claim to be tunable for practical use on smaller projects but, of course, I contend that this would be starting in the wrong place.

For a small low-risk project we need to start with the absolute minimum of documentation, and only add in one or two extra documents when we believe they will give us some advantage.

Most larger approaches to project management start at the fully-comprehensive position, and suggest that the project manager might leave out certain processes or document. I commend the method described in this book for use on ALL projects if the only alternative is to do nothing because you don't like the look of the bureaucracy in the alternative approaches.

The Relationship between PRINCE and SP method

About the Author

Mike Watson
MBCS, DMS, MAPM, PMP

Mike Watson has 20 years of experience in Information Technology, and a further 15 years spent as a consultant specialising in management training and consultancy assignments. He has taken a special interest in the personal skills of managing and working in teams.

His industry experience includes about 8 years working in Pharmaceuticals, both as an employee (Chief Programmer for the Wellcome Foundation) and as a consultant (project management consultant to Zeneca Pharmaceuticals). During these consultancy assignments, he implemented a project management methodology, trained all levels of personnel, and ran some special team training events for the medical staff on drug development teams.

He spent about 10 years in the financial services sector, on work assignments ranging from insurance to pensions.

As a project manager, he has managed a diverse range of mostly IT projects, ranging from large strategic systems developments through Internet and Intranet applications. He recently completed a range of global assignments at a world-class software company, travelling the world implementing best practices in running a Project Support Office.

In 1996, he designed and implemented a programme of training that won the Unisys award for 'most innovative IT training,' with the presentation of the award by the Secretary of State for education and Training in the Houses of Parliament in London.

He has been a speaker at many conferences and seminars, written numerous articles for professional journals, and this book, entitled 'Managing Smaller Projects,' which was originally published in January 1998, has become a best seller in its genre.

He was involved with the launch of the British Computer Society training programme for Programme and Project Support Office personnel.

He has a Diploma of Management Studies, is a full member of the British Computer Society, and the APM (the Association for Project Management), and has the prestigious qualification PMP (Project Management Professional) from the Project Management Institute.

He is a fellow of the Royal Society of the Arts, where he is engaged in supporting the manifesto challenge 'Developing a Capable Population.'

Mike Watson is practice leader of the Project Management Faculty of MCE (Management Centre Europe – the European arm of the American Management Association) in Brussels, and in his spare time is Managing Director of a software company in England, developing management and application software.

It is this last activity that brings the fun; for, as Mike says, 'running projects for profit concentrates the mind.'

Project Lessons from the Great Escape (Stalag Luft III)

While you might think your project plan is perfect, would you bet your life on it?

In World War II, a group of 220 captured airmen did just that -- they staked the lives of everyone in the camp on the success of a project to secretly build a series of long tunnels out of a prison camp their captors thought was escape proof.

The prisoners formally structured their work as a project, using the project organization techniques of the day. This book analyzes their efforts using modern project management methods and the nine knowledge areas from the *Guide to the Project Management Body of Knowledge* published by the Project Managment Institute. Learn from the successes and mistakes of a project where people really put their lives on the line.

ISBN: 1-895186-80-3   (paperback)
ISBN: 1-895186-81-1   (PDF ebook)

http://www.mmpubs.com/greatescape

Churchill's Adaptive Enterprise: *Lessons for Business Today*

This book analyzes a period of time from World War II when Winston Churchill, one of history's most famous leaders, faced near defeat for the British in the face of sustained German attacks. The book describes the strategies he used to overcome incredible odds and turn the tide on the impending invasion. The historical analysis is done through a modern business and information technology lens, describing Churchill's actions and strategy using modern business tools and techniques. Aimed at business executives, IT managers, and project managers, the book extracts learnings from Churchill's experiences that can be applied to business problems today. Particular themes in the book are knowledge management, information portals, adaptive enterprises, and organizational agility.

ISBN: 1-895186-19-6 (paperback)
ISBN: 1-895186-20-X (PDF ebook)

http://www.mmpubs.com/churchill

Titanic Lessons for IT Projects

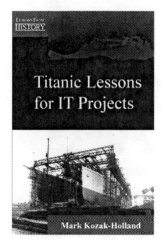

Titanic Lessons for IT Projects analyzes the project that designed, built, and launched the ship, showing how compromises made during early project stages led to serious flaws in this supposedly "perfect ship." In addition, the book explains how major mistakes during the early days of the ship's operations led to the disaster. All of these disasterous compromises and mistakes were fully avoidable.

Entertaining and full of intriguing historical details, this companion book to *Avoiding Project Disaster: Titanic Lessons for IT Executives* helps project managers and IT executives see the impact of decisions similar to the ones that they make every day. An easy read full of illustrations and photos to help explain the story and to help drive home some simple lessons.

ISBN: 1-895186-26-9 (paperback)
Also available in ebook formats.

http://www.mmpubs.com/titanic

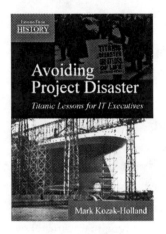

Avoiding Project Disaster: Titanic Lessons for IT Executives

Imagine you are in one of *Titanic's* lifeboats. As you look back at the wreckage site, you wonder how such a disaster could have happened. What were the causes? How could things have gone so badly wrong?

Titanic's maiden voyage was a disaster waiting to happen as a result of the compromises made in the project that constructed the ship. This book explores how modern executives can take lessons from a nuts-and-bolts construction project like *Titanic* and use those lessons to ensure the right approach to developing online business solutions. Looking at this historical project as a model will prove to be incisive as it cuts away the layers of IT jargon and complexity.

Avoiding Project Disaster is about delivering IT projects in a world where being on time and on budget is not enough. You also need to be up and running around the clock for your customers and partners. This book will help you successfully maneuver through the ice floes of IT management in an industry with a notoriously high project failure rate.

ISBN: 1-895186-73-0   (paperback)
Also available in ebook formats.

http://www.mmpubs.com/disaster

Edited by Kevin Aguanno, PMP, MAPM

The Project Management Essentials Library

Managing Agile Projects

Are you being asked to manage a project with unclear requirements, high levels of change, or a team using Extreme Programming or other Agile Methods?

If you are a project manager or team leader who is interested in learning the secrets of successfully controlling and delivering agile projects, then this is the book for you.

From learning how agile projects are different from traditional projects, to detailed guidance on a number of agile management techniques and how to introduce them onto your own projects, this book has the insider secrets from some of the industry experts – the visionaries who developed the agile methodologies in the first place.

ISBN: 1-895186-11-0   (paperback)
ISBN: 1-895186-12-9   (PDF ebook)

http://www.agilesecrets.com

Your wallet is empty? And you still need to boost your team's performance?

Building team morale is difficult in these tough economic times. Author Kevin Aguanno helps you solve the team morale problem with ideas for team rewards that won't break the bank.

Learn over 100 ways you can reward your project team and individual team members for just a few dollars. Full of innovative (and cheap!) ideas. Even with the best reward ideas, rewards can fall flat if they are not suitable to the person, the organization, the situation, or the magnitude of the accomplishment. Learn the four key factors that will *maximize* the impact of your rewards, and *guarantee* delighted recipients.

101 Ways to Reward Team Members for $20 (or Less!) teaches you how to improve employee morale, improve employee motivation, improve departmental and cross-organizational teaming, maximize the benefits of your rewards and recognition programme, and avoid the common mistakes.

ISBN: 1-895186-04-8   (paperback)
Also available in ebook formats. Order from your local bookseller, Amazon.com, or directly from the publisher at **http://www.mmpubs.com**

By Peter R. Garber

Want to Get Ahead in Your Career?

Do you find yourself challenged by office politics, bad things happening to good careers, dealing with the "big cheeses" at work, the need for effective networking skills, and keeping good working relationships with coworkers and bosses? *Winning the Rat Race at Work* is a unique book that provides you with case studies, interactive exercises, self-assessments, strategies, evaluations, and models for overcoming these workplace challenges. The book illustrates the stages of a career and the career choices that determine your future, empowering you to make positive changes.

Written by Peter R. Garber, the author of *100 Ways to Get on the Wrong Side of Your Boss*, this book is a must read for anyone interested in getting ahead in his or her career. You will want to keep a copy in your top desk drawer for ready reference whenever you find yourself in a challenging predicament at work.

ISBN: 1-895186-68-4 (paperback)
Also available in ebook formats. Order from your local bookseller, Amazon.com, or directly from the publisher at
http://www.mmpubs.com/rats

74 Tips
for *Absolutely Great*
Teleconference
Meetings

Ida Shessel

Become a meeting superstar!

With the proliferation of teleconference meetings in today's distributed team environment, many organizations now conduct most of their meetings over the telephone. There are challenges associated with trying to ensure that these meetings are productive and successful.

74 Tips for Absolutely Great Teleconference Meetings contains tips for both the teleconference leader and the participant — tips on how to prepare for the teleconference, start the teleconference meeting and set the tone, lead the teleconference, keep participants away from their e-mail during the call, use voice and language effectively, and draw the teleconference to a close. The book also includes a helpful checklist you can use to assess what you need to do to make your teleconference meetings more effective.

Mastering the art of holding a good meeting is one sure-fire way to get recognized as a leader by your peers and your management. Being able to hold an *absolutely great* teleconference meeting positions you as a leader who can also leverage modern technologies to improve efficiency. Develop this career-building skill by ordering this book today!

Available in electronic formats from most ebook online retailers or directly from the publisher at **www.mmpubs.com**.

Networking *for* Results

T H E   P O W E R   *O F*   P E R S O N A L   C O N T A C T

In partnership with Michael J. Hughes, *The* Networking Guru, Multi-Media Publications Inc. has released a new series of books, ebooks, and audio books designed for business and sales professionals who want to get the most out of their networking events and help their career development.

Networking refers to the concept that each of us has a group or "network" of friends, associates and contacts as part of our on-going human activity that we can use to achieve certain objectives.

The *Networking for Results* series of products shows us how to think about networking strategically, and gives us step-by-step techniques for helping ourselves and those around us achieve our goals. By following these practices, we can greatly improve our personal networking effectiveness.

Visit **www.Networking-for-Results.com** for information on specific products in this series, to read free articles on networking skills, or to sign up for a free networking tips newsletter. Products are available from most book, ebook, and audiobook retailers, or directly from the publisher at **www.mmpubs.com**.

 **The Project Management
Audio Library**

In a recent CEO survey, the leaders of today's largest corporations identified project management as the top skillset for tomorrow's leaders. In fact, many organizations place their top performers in project management roles to groom them for senior management positions. Project managers represent some of the busiest people around. They are the ones responsible for planning, executing, and controlling most major new business activities.

Expanding upon the successful *Project Management Essentials Library* series of print and electronic books, Multi-Media Publications has launched a new imprint called the *Project Management Audio Library.* Under this new imprint, MMP is publishing audiobooks and recorded seminars focused on professionals who manage individual projects, portfolios of projects, and strategic programmes. The series covers topics including agile project management, risk management, project closeout, interpersonal skills, and other related project management knowledge areas.

This is not going to be just the "same old stuff" on the critical path method, earned value, and resource levelling; rather, the series will have the latest tips and techniques from those who are at the cutting edge of project management research and real-world application.

www.PM-Audiobooks.com

Printed in the United States
65239LVS00002B/250-279